Praise for

Learning as If Life Depended on It

This is the best book I have read about education, ever. This is in part because it refuses to be a book bounded by education: it shows how thinking seriously about education for a thriving humanity entails exploring much more broadly and deeply the nature of our predicament, in all its complexity. Deeply grounded in philosophy, no simplistic models or fixes are proposed; but the transformation in thinking that is required is laid out with crystalline clarity. This is a book that is unafraid to ground the education debate in concepts such as wisdom, love, and the mystery of humanity. It is beautifully written, akin on occasion to poetry. That it comes from a former politician and practising system leader makes it all the more miraculous.
Valerie Hannon, Author of THRIVE: *The Purpose of Schools in a Changing World*

Reading Olli-Pekka Heinonen's book felt like coming home to a truth I have long sensed but seldom seen articulated with such clarity and grace: that the future of education is not about more technology or more information, but about reconnecting with the deepest essence of what it means to learn, to grow, to become fully human in a rapidly evolving world. Heinonen's vision is at once sobering and inspiring — he unflinchingly confronts the illusions and missed targets of our current educational paradigm, while also illuminating the boundless possibilities that emerge when we bring learning into synergy with the organic unfolding of life itself. His seamless integration of cutting-edge science with enduring universal principles is a model for the kind of whole-system thinking

that our times demand. His book is an essential companion to midwife a new story of learning that is holistic, regenerative, and congruent with the needs of the 21st century. May this luminous work inspire a rising generation of solutionaries who will lead us towards a thriving future.
Francis Cholle, Founder and CEO of the Know Better World Foundation

Required reading for anyone who cares about the future of humanity ... masterfully explores the great challenges and misperceptions that shape our world, urging us to rethink how we approach learning, human potential, and societal progress.
Vikas Pota, Executive Chairman, Education Leaders Forum

Civilisation is under threat. Large numbers of people who are thoughtful, ethical, and brave are required to protect it. Education ought to be the incubator of such people. Educationists who can see clearly what's needed and show schools the way back to their fundamental purpose are in short supply — but Olli-Pekka Heinonen has emerged as the leader of this small but crucial pack. In this wise, lucid, and heartfelt book, he offers us hope and direction, not just for the regeneration of education, but for the preservation of our planetary home.
Professor Guy Claxton, author of *The Future of Teaching and the Myths That Hold It Back*

Olli-Pekka Heinonen's eloquent and well-structured book offers us an exceptionally profound analysis of the root causes of the wicked problems mankind is collectively facing today. He demonstrates convincingly how these problems can't be solved by doing more of the same faster and more efficiently

— or with brute force — but require thoroughly new ways of thinking and acting — at individual and collective levels.
Mikko Kosonen, Chairman of Kordelin Foundation

Learning as If Life Depended on It provides a rare and profound shared vision that connects a collective learning consciousness ... It is a guidebook that reflects on the dilemmas of an ambiguous world and the ability to deal with it ... The book explores learning from the intimate to the ultimate.
Dr. Ameeta Mulla Wattal, Chairperson and Executive Director, DLF Scholarship Programmes and Schools

Heinonen finds profound answers to how humans can build the agency, co-agency and collective agency to close the disconnect between the accelerating revolution of our social and cultural environment, and our biological capacity to adapt. It provides a novel and truly eye-opening perspective on learning as a deeply ethical process of being and becoming human.
Andreas Schleicher, Director for Education and Skills, Organisation for Economic Co-operation and Development (OECD)

At a time when daily experience suggests that our governance systems are failing or are being pushed beyond their design tolerances with practices that are morally and ethically questionable, it is uplifting to find inspiration for another world 'that could be' through the writings and reflections of Olli-Pekka Heinonen, former State Secretary to the Prime Minister of Finland. Olli-Pekka rightly alludes to the Finnish saying: 'it is time for the cat to stop circling the hot porridge!' in outlining the imperatives facing humanity. Fortunately, he has a track record that demonstrates through his ideas

and his actions that transformation in what we do when we do what we do is both feasible and possible. This book is grounded in his experiences of systemic governing. It can be read in the conviction that all that is said is doable! In this excellent, readable book, Olli-Pekka offers new systemic insights (e.g., escaping 10 illusions that trap us in outdated mental models) through which we can all lay down new pathways of hope in our living in relationship with each other, with our planet and with other species.
Professor Ray Ison, President of the International Federation for Systems Research

Spanning complexity, crisis management, and knowledge wars, *Learning as If Life Depended on It* challenges us to nothing less than understanding how to be human in our own time. How might we shift away from being "overtrained and undereducated" to building mechanisms for shared wisdom and authentic learning? A deeply reflective and thought-provoking read.
Tracey Burns, Chief of Global Strategy and Research, National Center on Education and the Economy

Learning as If Life Depended on It is a timely and essential read. With both clarity and depth, Olli-Pekka Heinonen offers a panoramic view of today's global challenges and humanity's place within them. He argues that the profound issues we face demand a fundamental shift in how we learn and engage with one another. Olli-Pekka invites us to reimagine education — not as a tool for competition but as a path back to wisdom, ethics, and shared human values. In a world increasingly defined by complexity and fragmentation, this book is a powerful reminder that our future depends on collective learning, global responsibility, and the flourishing of all — not just the individual. It's both a call to action and a source of hope for navigating the path ahead.

Michaela Horvathova, Co-founder and Chief Education Officer at Beyond Education

Immerse yourself in this truly remarkable exploration of a viable future for humanity. You will emerge with a fierce desire to develop your own human potential and to more deeply invest in your fellow humans — with renewed purpose.

Anthony Mackay AM, Board Chair, National Center on Education & the Economy, Washington DC

Learning as If Life Depended on It

Learning as If Life Depended on It

Why We Must See the World Anew, and Figure Out What Follows

by Olli-Pekka Heinonen

English translation by Eva Malkki, adapted and edited by Perspectiva Press and Tim Logan, in consultation with the author.

PERSPECTIVA

First published by Perspectiva Press, 2025
An imprint of Perspectiva (trading name of Perspectives on Systems, Souls and Society, a UK-registered charity no. 1170492)
London
www.systems-souls-society.com

For distributor details and how to order please email greetings@perspectiva.co.uk

Text copyright: Olli-Pekka Heinonen, 2025

ISBN: 978 1 914568 07 7
978 1 914568 08 4 (ebook)

All rights reserved. Except for brief quotations in critical articles or reviews, no part of this book may be reproduced in any manner without prior written permission from the publishers.

The rights of Olli-Pekka Heinonen as author have been asserted in accordance with the Copyright, Designs and Patents Act 1988.

A CIP catalogue record for this book is available from the British Library.

English translation by Eva Malkki, from the original Finnish text, *Eletään ihmisiksi – Yhteisöllistä viisautta etsimässä* by Olli-Pekka Heinonen.

The English translation was adapted and edited by Perspectiva Press and Tim Logan, in close collaboration with the author, to reshape the structure and expression for a new readership.

Design: Lapiz Digital Services

Illustrations and cover design by Christopher Burrows

UK: Printed and bound by CPI Group (UK) Ltd, Croydon, CR0 4YY

The manufacturer's authorised representative in the EU for product safety is: eucomply OÜ – Pärnu mnt 139b-14, 11317 Tallinn, Estonia, hello@eucompliancepartner.com, www.eucompliancepartner.com

Contents

Appreciation and Gratitude	xiii

Introduction
How Can We Ensure That Future Generations Enjoy the Miracle of Life? 1

Part One: Predicament

The Map Is Failing the Territory	13
Information Is Not the Friend It Used to Be	23
Old Language Stifles New Worlds	27
Precious Achievements Are Unreasonably Brittle	33
Progress Casts a Long Shadow	37
The Idea of Problems Is Problematic	43
Risks Are Agglomerating	45
Confusion Is Justified	51
We Do Not Seem to Know How to Know	57
We Fail to See Ourselves as Predators	61

Part Two: Perception

The Illusion of Simplicity	77
The Illusion of Control	87
The Illusion of Divisibility	93
The Illusion of Competition	101
The Illusion of Technocracy	107
The Illusion of Graduation	111
The Illusion of Anthropocentrism	115
The Illusion of Knowing	119
The Illusion of Relativism	129
The Illusion of Permanence	133

Part Three: Potential

We Are in the Unseen	143

We Are with the Unknown	147
We Are Our Shared Uniqueness	149
We Are the Ever-Present Ending	155
We Are the Others We Don't Know	159
We Are Our Rituals and Routines	161
We Are Ongoing Creation	163
We Are Our Sensitivities	167
We Are Our Expanding Perspectives	169
We Are Systems Learning	173
We Are Uniformity and Diversity	179
We Are Democracies Learning to Renew Democracy	181
We Are Reimagining Governance for a Planetary Context	185
We Are the One and the Many	191

Part Four: Pathways

Learning as Adaptive Advantage	199
Learning as Prefigurative Culture	203
Learning as Relating	207
Learning as Predicting the Unpredictable	211
Learning as Collective Development	215
Learning as Dialogue	219
Learning as Autonomy and Trust	225
Learning as Self-direction	231
Learning as Leadership	235
Learning as Universal Imperative	243
Learning as Global Ethic	247
Learning as a Journey into Ourselves	251

Epilogue:

Global Challenges as Educational Challenges	261

Bibliography 269

Appreciation and Gratitude

THIS BOOK was written with my children, Iiro, Saara, and Oskari, on top of my mind. To write about the threats of the world that we have created, and the despair it brings, made it painful for me to comprehend that I am talking about *their* future. But that only brought speed to my pen to move towards the hope on the other side of despair; hope to do the right thing as a duty. I am so thankful to my children that I can be their father, and now a grandfather for the first time.

My wife Taina was always patient and supportive, even when two months of holiday and relaxed writing, to finalise the original Finnish version of the book, suddenly shifted to 3 weeks of work around the clock to get it done. And I am always thankful for her for being my muse.

The idea to have a translated version of the book came from people I had the great fortune to meet in international education who would ask, "When can we read the book in English?". However, that still wasn't enough for me to engage with the idea, but it needed key people to believe in the book and its message. Tim Logan was such a person. Without his ability to make the dream a reality, this book would not be here. I would also like to thank the team at Perspectiva Press, Jonathan Rowson, Kylen Preator and Leigh Biddlecome for bringing the book to life in good shape. And sincere thanks to Eva Malkki for the excellent translation work; and Christopher Burrows, for the beautiful illustrations and cover art.

Everything I have written I have learned from others. To have thought partners from prior centuries, who feel closer to you than your neighbours, is the great gift that literacy gives us. I am a small person on the shoulders of the giants, but I would be a fool not to use the view they offer me. These great people are not just the familiar names from history, but also the connection to my ancestors – like my grandmothers, with whom I spent a lot of time in my youth. They showed me how to strive to live a good and humble life. And my parents, who created the conditions to inspire in me a curious and open mind towards all people, and the model of hard work to do your share.

I have been lucky to have such caring and insightful people in my life, expressing their creativity through a rich variety of languages – music, sports, media, education, leadership, politics, religion, governance, and human growth as a connecting thread from youth to today. If they read this, they know I am talking about them.

Finally, to give credit to where it belongs, most of the ideas in this book surfaced for me while immersed in nature. The Finnish forest, the seaside, the vast grain fields. They have contributed to this book as much as I have. Those are the places where I feel at home; where my heartbeat calms down and my mind opens up.

Introduction
How Can We Ensure That Future Generations Enjoy the Miracle of Life?

M Y MAIN motivation in writing this book was to try to understand what it means to be human in our era, and how we can ensure that future generations enjoy the miracle of life. I had been Minister in three different governments for eight years, during which time Finland joined the European Union and took steps to becoming the leading country in information and communication technology, and education. I had seen the national agenda through the lens of being Television Director in the Finnish Public Service Media Company, YLE. I had experienced the challenges of national decision-making as State Secretary in the Prime Minister's Office and several other ministries. And I had seen how a diversifying and polarising society changes the dynamics and identity of schools and teachers, as the Director General of the National Agency for Education.

I was privileged to have these vantage points for 30 years in Finnish society, and as a result, I began to see deep and slow movements that worried me. They were not unique to Finland but were global trends having a strong impact on a country characterised by high levels of trust, equality and stability.

Seeing the depths of the strongest impacts of the Covid-19 pandemic was the particular moment in which the book, in its original Finnish, came into being – a global pause to reflect on the directions in which we were collectively heading. However, since then, we have witnessed mostly a 'bounce-back' form of societal resilience, rather than the transformative resilience that many of us hoped for, to better position ourselves to face other known and unknown crises into the future.

Sadly, we have also seen the toxic cocktail I describe in the book become even more dangerous. The overlapping nature of different crises has shown where it can lead. The war in Europe made it a realistic possibility of sending my own children to war. The unparalleled rise of advanced artificial intelligence, fuelled by fierce competition for more innovative applications, has given little time to care about the wider implications for humankind and about the global institutions necessary to maintain alignment with values.

As both cause and consequence of these changes, the greatest worry to me personally as a father, as a Finn, and as a human being, is the accelerated deterioration of trust: trust between individuals, throughout societies and across the globe. The power structures and ideologies based on game-theoretic competition between weakening nation states and a few strengthening global companies winning it all, have created a dynamic which is deeply disruptive of the trust in our ability, as citizens of this planet, to create a better world.

However, I am also fascinated by the way in which, following the second world war, we successfully drew on our collective capacity to respond to crisis. Through vital cooperation, we were able to create global institutions and decision-making processes to clean up the mess after the war. We rebuilt trust with transparent processes that enabled humankind to take a step forward. My deepest hope is that we do the same today, without global warfare. Clearly, the solutions need to be very different from the Bretton Woods agreements. But similar is the ability to imagine new social technologies, ideals, and constructs, which will enable us all to live peacefully with ourselves, others, including the future generations, and with the planet.

Change in my own professional life has taken me to those same roots of Bretton Woods. At that time, much thought was being given to what kind of education would be needed to ensure that the horrors of WWII would never happen again. Those wise people imagined an education programme that would lead to the development of the International Baccalaureate, which I have the honour to lead today. It has grown into a truly global education system, with programmes in 159 countries and almost 6000 schools.

The mission of IB is to develop inquiring, knowledgeable and caring young people who help to create a better and more peaceful world through education that builds intercultural understanding and respect. With everything I have written in this book prior to joining the IB, it should be obvious to the reader that I am living my dream to play my part in making a difference.

The ideas I present here are products of interaction – just as all ideas are, however much we might want to claim authorship. The other party to those interactions might have lived 2500 years ago and written a poem, or be alive now and have sat at a round table with me; they may have played music or engaged me in a conversation on a train that felt meaningful in the here and now.

In writing this book, I have been shored up and accompanied by all of those contributors.

My main realisations have been fuelled by the fact that similar phenomena have come up in different contexts, disciplines, spheres of life, sectors of government and realms of experience. Artistic performances, scientific articles or day-to-day discussions at school may all tackle the same phenomena, despite using different terminology. These experiences have led me to believe that something larger and more significant is under way.

Naturally it may be a case of confirmation bias: just me noticing the things that I have been delving into myself, and observing reality through that lens – like a couple trying for a baby who notice prams everywhere. It could be me hearing myself in the echo chamber in which we all spend much of our time. However, these are the patterns I am perceiving, and I share them with humility and a curiosity to continue learning.

When you have been involved in politics, you realise that politicianship brands you permanently. From that time on, some people will view everything you say and do as a manifestation of that brand. Your thoughts and what you stand for are either good or evil, depending on whether or not you belong to the same ideological grouping as the beholder.

Therefore I feel it important to state that this book is not linked to any party political ideology or discourse. I have tried to attain a meta-political level that allows me to examine the norms and explicit or implicit rules on which politics is based.

I have on numerous occasions found myself in situations where top political decision-makers, right up to the Prime Minister, have had visions of what should be done and how, but have discovered that in reality politics does not allow for it. Each of these occasions has shattered a small part of the idealism that the persons in question originally brought into their careers, and has taken them closer to a situation in which playing the game according to existing rules becomes an end in itself – an iron cage that narrows the horizon for dreams and opportunities of change. *[handwritten annotation: Weber: Iron Cage!]*

At the end, all that is left is that iron cage and the remaining players' battle for dominance. The rules of the game of politics should be examined critically, so that we can find mechanisms for changing them, to better serve our purposes. History offers us examples of revolutions, but they are too drastic, on the one hand, and too superficial, on the other, to effect a proper change of norms.

If I have not worn my politician's hat in writing this book, neither have I worn that of the Director General of the Finnish National Board of Education or of the International Baccalaureate, or any other role I have held. This book is not about education policy, because I could – and, perhaps one day, will – write a whole other tome on that topic.

The mystery of humanity can never be expressed in words. It is beyond verbalisation. Still, words are one of the best methods that we have for sharing that mystery; touch, facial expressions and shared feelings may come closer, but their sphere of influence is narrower than that of language. Thinking and expressing thoughts through language are natural ways of being human for me. This book is my contribution to trying to make the world a better place.

Writing a book involves challenging oneself. Questioning my own thinking has been ever present, but so has my faith in the idea that relying on the uniqueness of our life experiences and history is the best that each of us can bring to the shared table. The process was a test of whether I could form my thoughts into a cohesive worldview on the individual, communal and global levels. Whether what I was writing was synchronised with how I act and think, writing is a journey into oneself.

This book does not provide detailed, intricate models or concrete solutions to society's problems. There is a reason for that. I have tried to make the book consistent with its core messages. I do not believe in ready-made solutions presented by individuals to other individuals. Broad-based leadership and ownership of collective responses generate the joint commitment that the challenges of our time require. In that sense, the process of communal learning and wisdom is more important than certain, time-specific solutions.

This book consists of four parts. I begin by attempting to describe the **predicament** of our times. People's lives involve a huge variety of issues, and there is no scarcity of challenges when it comes to societies, either. I want to focus on the challenges that we face in terms of being human and surviving – thriving – as a species. Second, I draw attention to ten illusions, which cloud our **perceptions** of our predicament and prevent us finding sustainable ways out. Third, I consider our **potential** but also what might need to change for such a way out to be viable. Finally, I suggest answers as to what learning and models of action might create **pathways** to forms of cohabitation and interaction that would produce better results. I examine these responses on four levels: the individual, the local community (including our workplaces), the society and the globe.

A note on the use of the word 'we'
While I don't profess to speak on behalf of others whose lived experiences I do not have, I use the collective pronoun 'we' very intentionally to denote a unifying species-level solidarity. My motivation to write this book surfaced from some gloomy projections of how things could go badly wrong for us. However,

Introduction

I am more optimistic than ever about our capacity as authentic individuals to come together and enact our full, collective humanity. We must behave like the humans we truly are, as the original Finnish title of this book – "Let's be Human!" implored us to do.

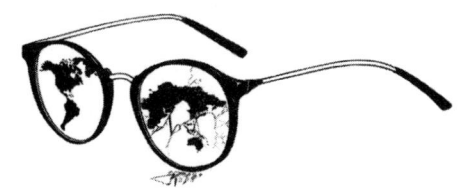

Part One: Predicament

Q: What do we most need to understand?

A: Humanity is suffering from an identity crisis. Our worldview is out of tune with reality. Our mental models need updating.

1. *The Map Is Failing the Territory*
2. *Information Is Not the Friend It Used to Be*
3. *Old Language Stifles New Worlds*
4. *Precious Achievements Are Unreasonably Brittle*
5. *Progress Casts a Long Shadow*
6. *The Idea of Problems Is Problematic*
7. *Risks Are Agglomerating*
8. *Confusion Is Justified*
9. *We Do Not Seem to Know How to Know*
10. *We Fail to See Ourselves as Predators*

"Unreal!" This exclamation, at one time heard repeatedly from the mouths of my children, echoes in my head. The word, with an emphasis on the *real*, would be their reaction to any odd or surprising occurrence.

Increasingly often, I come across events or news that seem unreal, and I notice that I am not alone in this sentiment. What is real in our time? How do we know what is real and what can be trusted? Who possesses the authority to define reality?

When I was writing the Finnish-language version of this book, the Covid-19 crisis cloaked the future in a mist of uncertainty. Restrictions on personal freedoms and bans on physical interaction impacted people's basic needs. As the pandemic dragged on, it resulted in a kind of trauma, a loss of control over one's own life. Recovering from trauma takes time and affects our disposition towards the future, gnawing at our hope and faith. The sense of uncertainty has remained and will remain with us long after the Covid crisis has faded, and every new crisis – large or small – is likely to bring back memories of it.

There is no indication that we will be spared from future startling and unexpected events. The world appears permanently to have shifted to a nonlinear and unpredictable nature. We should prepare for an era of uncertainty.

There is still a vast majority of people in the world who believe that we can maintain our living standards while avoiding the difficulties that are predicted to follow from climate change, the mass extinction of species, and biodiversity loss. I no longer believe that. Keeping up our existing ways of living and thinking will mean journeying towards unprecedented suffering. Either we decide how to take hold of it, or it will overtake us as an unbridled torrent of crises, including the political emergencies and violence that we are starting to see.

Another alternative exists. The pandemic demonstrated that, if need be, people and humanity can change certain principles and behaviours that were once regarded as sacred or enduring. The experience can help us to envisage how we could gently redirect our materialistic Western society and philosophy, which are steeped in rationality and competitiveness, towards a more holistic and philanthropic understanding. We must adapt to a changing environment by redefining ourselves.

The Map Is Failing the Territory

I RECALL my grandmother following the news of the fire storm caused by falling bombs in the Vietnam War on her black-and-white television set. Her concern was that that reality could soon reach her in her tiny, peaceful village in Western Finland. Even as a child, I realised that granny was mixing up TV reality with her own reality.

Today's world is different. International crises will quickly reach around the entire world. A virus that originated in the city of Wuhan took only a few months to reach every corner of the world and to shift reality in all aspects of life. Earlier, the financial crisis sparked by mortgage lending in the US tore a lasting rupture into distant economies.

Good things also spread quickly, however. *#MeToo* and discussions on racial stereotyping have made visible some of the repressive structures in many cultures, leading to the emergence of healing processes. Children and young people around the world have followed others' examples in taking climate action, helping to defuse some of their climate anxiety through concrete deeds.

The ubiquity of transportation and data communications, alongside globalised economies and increased human mobility, has created dense networks among people. The subsequent increase in interdependence has brought us all face to face with the same challenges and phenomena.

The increase in media content and the sharing nature of social media have influenced our ways of understanding reality. For instance, Covid-19 was not only a pandemic but also a so-called infodemic, which refers to the spreading of huge amounts of information quickly to a vast amount of people. Both true and false data linked to this one topic were directed in unprecedented volumes at practically every person around the world.

The fact that the media on offer have become diversified has not meant a diversification in its demand. To some extent the opposite has been true: it is possible to consume an increasingly narrow segment of the increasingly broad supply, and to live within the bubble that that creates. We can escape the complexity of the world by viewing it through our chosen keyhole.

"Everything flows, nothing stands still," said the philosopher Heraclitus over two millennia ago. Today, many of us feel that the flow has accelerated. We are swept away by the stream, and our fear of losing control at any moment is growing. And this current is not unidirectional – it pulls us this way and that, obscuring any steady horizon. We are so caught in fighting the current and trying to keep our heads above water that we cannot discern purpose, let alone move with conviction. Our will cannot be fulfilled in the maelstrom.

How can we make sense of what is happening in the world and what is significant and pertinent? How can we maintain our functional ability amid overarching, complex change? How can we distinguish the things we can personally affect from those which lie outside of our sphere of influence? How can we preserve our mental integrity as the world splinters around us? How can we *be human* in our own time?

I want to try to figure out what is real. Reality is shaped by what draws our attention – and we tend to notice what matters to us. This, in turn, is strongly linked to our agency: our ability, willingness and opportunity to make choices.

Even in Finland, trying to evaluate society's status quo is like looking at a running river. From afar, it appears to flow peacefully and steadily. We are internationally admired, topping many comparison charts and being used as examples of how certain things should be done. Observed close up, the image is different: there are torrents and spumes, splatters and splashes, with various whirlpools and currents pulling in all directions. Both experiences are true and neither entitles us to ignore the other.

I have usually been more concerned by the close-up picture. This may be a vestige of my life in the early 1990s when, practically straight out of university, I was able to observe the tottering Finnish economy right at the edge of the abyss, as the then Minister of Finance, Iiro Viinanen, put it. He could not publicly discuss everything he knew about the proximity of the edge.

Again we stand close to the edge, but the scale of the abyss is different. We are not looking at a single nation's economy but at sustaining favourable living conditions for humanity and life on Earth. Unlike Viinanen, who felt compelled to hide the seriousness of the situation, thousands of scientists have been proclaiming the news based on scientific evidence for years. The question is: do we hear them? If we do, what should we be doing differently? How can we bring about change?

The world that spreads itself before us does not fit with our internal worldviews. It is a compatibility clash. The world has quickly assumed a shape whose demands cannot be met by our traditional individual and communal abilities. Our external reality has characteristics that feel strange and wrong to many people, to the point that their mental health is shaken.

We are like coastal flowers transplanted into the mountains. In a changed environment, a flower species usually cannot thrive and may wilt away completely. The flower's ability to adapt to a new ecosystem is not fast enough.

Humans differ from plants in that we can change our own environments and adapt to new ones. Even the world that now no longer fits our worldview was made by us. It follows that we could similarly create a new kind of reality. The cultural evolution that is continuously taking place through our actions affects the circumstances in which biological evolution takes place. Biology deals the cards and culture plays the hand it has. We are simultaneously creators and creations.

The challenges of our internal and external worlds are closely linked. Global issues demand that we re-evaluate our mental models and deep-seated beliefs. The strength of humans lies in the fact that we are able to quickly adapt to new circumstances by learning. And that is what we must now do.

According to Brian Walsh (Walsh & Middleton, 1984) and Clifford Geertz (1977), a worldview consists of two elements: a model of the world and a model for acting in that world. An individual is an agent in the world, and the world is an arena for the individual's actions. The compatibility of the two elements becomes a crucial issue.

The map of our worldview is, at least partly, subconscious; beyond our conscious efforts to adjust it, it directs our life choices, reactions and emotions. The map is drawn from infancy onwards, following our life experiences. The frames for the map come from our heredity and are moulded by evolution, and they influence the marks that our experiences will make. All this shapes our understanding of ourselves, our relationships with others, what is real and how the world works.

We see reality within the scope of our individual worldviews; this means that we miss some of the things that happen because they fall outside of the frames of our map. In the perceivable world, we look for signs that correspond to our worldview. We are keen to find them and we jump on them like a tourist seeking the right street name.

When reality presents us with events that clash with our worldviews, we react in diverse ways. Any conflict between reality and our worldview creates stress.

Documentarist Virpi Suutari investigated a popular phone-in programme on Finnish public radio ("Kansanradio", YLE) and in the process listened to a huge number of opinion phone calls made by the general public. Suutari explained (Virkkula, 2021):

> *For me, the predominant emotion that was conveyed was confusion. The feeling you get when things aren't how they were before, and you no longer know how to behave or what to think.*

Our quality of life and well-being depend to a great extent on how we act and cope in such situations.

A worldview could be described as a cultural manifestation of a biological ecosystem. An organism and its ecological niche have adapted to each other and are in continuous mutual interaction. A shark may be the king of the ocean, but drop it onto the savanna and it won't survive very long. It might, in fact, end up as dinner for that environment's king, the lion. We humans have turned the whole world into our ecological niche. We have learnt to cope with highly diverse conditions, from sweltering deserts to frozen poles. We cannot survive alone, of course: we thrive thanks to the protection afforded by community, and we spread widely thanks to our cultural development.

The future is a foreign country and culture for each of us. How can we prepare for it? The challenge could be compared to driving a car in a strange land: the road signs are unfamiliar, the steering wheel might be on the wrong side, there is too much traffic and we can't predict how others will behave. We can find out certain things before we travel, but most realities will be impossible to prepare for until we are actually there. It is only behind the wheel that you realise that you can't plan ahead in detail, because the people in the other cars don't know – or respect – your plan. The best thing to do is to be alert to your surroundings, to draw conclusions and thereby to learn to act and cope with the situation. Let the surrounding reality show you the next stage of your journey.

The concept of the worldview is often linked to the idea of what we desire from reality. In fact, our worldview strongly influences how we see the world "as it is". It determines what we define as significant and therefore what we pay attention to. Our attention delimits what we see and how the world presents itself to us "as it is". In his book *Thinking, Fast and Slow* (2011), Daniel Kahneman describes this cognitive bias using the term *WYSIATI*: "what you see is all there is".

Our worldview also becomes concretely embodied in how we modify our environment. An agrarian society's worldview differs from a modern, industrialised one, just as a countryside community's structure differs from a contemporary urban one. Environments mould the people that live in them. At the same time, we define what kinds of work, technologies and philosophies constitute "appropriate" modifications of the environment.

As individuals, we formulate our worldviews with the aim of creating a picture that is clear, feels right and works in practice. It must correspond sufficiently to "reality" for us to cope with situations we encounter, and to predict future situations. New events and learning experiences alter our unique models of the world.

The culture in which we are brought up strongly influences the worldview we hold to be ours and "true". Even if we want to distance ourselves or rebel against the worldview of our surroundings, it is still an anchor that majorly influences how we act.

These days it increasingly happens that the reality in which the worldview in our heads was drawn differs from the one where we find ourselves. The map and the landscape do not match; the map's symbols fail to give us essential information on the location of the next checkpoints.

How did we end up here? A worldview is a tool for coping with each operating environment as it arises. A hunter-gatherer's worldview was not tied to a physical location and did not require careful future planning or forecasting. As agriculture began to prevail, it brought the future into play, in the form of storage and commitment to a physical dwelling place. Religions created a communal authority of truth that established hierarchies for both secular and spiritual questions. Nation-states eventually took over responsibility for secular issues, laying down broader, shared rules of play. The scientific worldview emphasised the intellect and the individual's ability to understand reality through scientific reasoning and experimentation.

In our time, we are in touch with all these temporal layers: they blend and overlap, manifesting in new ways. Postmodern times have raised emotions and intuition to be alongside reason in significance, and has made us strive for a more comprehensive, all-embracing way of seeing things.

Now, once again, global challenges require us to shift our worldview so that we might better solve them. The friction between the latest crises and the previous layers of worldviews is evident on a daily basis in traditional and social media.

Religious viewpoints have lost some of their import in globalised Western societies. Many people no longer feel that they offer methods for understanding the fundamental questions in life, or suitable rituals for processing them. As information and cultural sharing have become more widely available, the diverse moral structures of the world are also within reach. We can pick and choose the ones that best suit each situation. Nationality, citizenship, morals, cultural and ethnic backgrounds, personal values: they are no longer confined to geographical boundaries. Estonia's idea of the digital society ("e-Estonia") has detached even nationhood from geography, offering e-residency to global citizens, allowing them to establish businesses and access digital services without ever setting foot in the country.

What was once clear and simple has become complex, and this causes tension and discord. This means that the need for communication and dialogue is heightened, but unfortunately our ability to carry these out constructively has weakened.

Perhaps the time for striving for a consistent, singular worldview is over, and we must accept diversity and adaptability, even at the individual level. This situation is new and requires that we comprehensively re-evaluate our worldviews. We are in an interim state between two realities: we still have access to the building blocks of our former worldview, but we cannot fashion them into a viable abode. We have had little practice in the use of newer building materials, and are still arguing over where to lay the foundations.

The world manifests itself as liquid, constantly flowing, so that it cannot be grasped. Our scientific–technological worldview has received blows in the whirlwind of postmodern information relativity and context-specificity, and it has been splintered into several mutually conflicting views. We cannot find the solid ground of a cohesive worldview to stand on in our time.

There is no dearth of utopias, i.e. visions of ideal conditions. In contrast, coming up with a method for journeying from the status quo to those ideal conditions is a terrifying challenge. Utopias are like meta-level answers to questions that were unanswerable in the first place. In each situation and moment, we are dealing with paradoxes that cannot be solved – that resist any solution. As people, we must grow if we want to find a bearable balance on the pivoting arms of the scales. The best utopias can help to clarify the desired direction of progress, but they can never know the necessary process of growth.

Therefore we do not need better utopias, but rather a process that will help us make meaningful progress. In a world with so much talk of global problems, surprisingly little is said about the methods for dealing with them. Awareness is not enough to generate change; decisions do not in themselves bring about the desired results. Something else is needed, and that is what I try to explore in this book. We must find a path on the narrow passage between order and chaos. Achieving that is known as wisdom.

Information Is Not the Friend It Used to Be

THROUGH HISTORY, worldviews have been examined from at least three perspectives: 1) the internal world of humans, 2) the collective culture and social imagination we have created and 3) reality as described through the natural sciences. These perspectives largely correspond to philosopher Karl Popper's theory of the three worlds (1978). Historically these perspectives have often been viewed separately, and diverse eras have been classified according to the perspective that was dominant at the time. Currently, all three perspectives are in flux.

Our internal mental coherence is being tested. Our propensity towards depression grows when there is a conflict between our external and internal demands, and our minds and selves are under duress. There is a risk of losing the connection between the internal and the external, which is exactly what happens with depression. Mental health issues are multiplying globally.

Our man-made shared cultural mechanisms are in trouble. The ethics we developed in small communities, which aims for the good of the many in the long term, does not seem to hold at the national and international levels. Democracy and the market economy are now being questioned and don't seem to be guiding us in the right direction. We have failed to develop a communal ethic or identity on a global scale. The well-being of the natural world has become caught up in rivalry between countries. The tensions that arise from this expose us, as a species, to communal trauma.

The scientific worldview has failed to meet the high expectations set for it by the Enlightenment and by our belief in scientific and technological progress. It offers no answers to the ultimate questions concerning humanity or to understanding how societies work.

There was a time when access to information was a bottleneck. Now the gates of information, knowledge and the related stimuli have been thrown wide open, and supply greatly surpasses demand. What is the new bottleneck? There is so much flow of information that we will drown unless we are able to swallow it in suitable mouthfuls. When there is a surfeit of information, the limiting factor is the way in which we manage our attention and our minds. Attention management is each of our own private medium: we each decide what contents we want to release into our awareness on each day.

At the same time, the world's top psychologists, brain researchers and service designers have been harnessed to hijack our willpower, to distract us from holding on to our choices and switch our attention to whatever the advertisers or app developers choose. The focus has shifted from information sharing to distracting our minds. Many digital applications reward us for lacking mind control, rather than reinforcing it. We have created a world that ruthlessly makes use of the weaknesses of our minds. This is why we now need inner peacekeepers.

We think of social media platforms as blackboards on which we write so that others may see what we are thinking. A blackboard is a static platform for publishing a message, and social media could actually not be further from this: they are platforms infused with a strong motivation and endeavour to use what we post for their own purposes. The tech giants' databases know more about us than we do ourselves.

They use that data for profit, selling it for commercial purposes and further processing. The more we use various platforms and applications, the higher the gain; encouraging social media dependency is financially profitable. We become dependent on things when we lack a connection with ourselves and replace it with an alternative function. On social media, we feel accepted when we receive likes, subscriptions and followers. When we are dependent on something, our ability to think independently and critically is impaired.

Simultaneously, we have polluted our information ecosystem. Our shared concept of reality has become fragmented and, in a very short period, knowledge and truth have become relative. The latest academic findings fade into simple points of view that may be called into question by a differing opinion. Experts' views shrink into something that can be bypassed by those with power. We have lost our shared trust in what is true and false.

Previously, we could tell false information apart from scientific data just by looking at it. That is no longer the case, even if we believe it to be so. Disinformation looks just as genuine, competent and high quality as evidence-based fact. Therefore, we are more likely to fall for information that does not come from research but is intended to push a certain agenda. We love to share information that we come across that looks credible, and it is easy for us to do so. When information is extensively shared, more people are likely to encounter it more often, i.e. that information becomes replicated. Repetition is known to be an effective way to increase the plausibility and reliability of information: something that propagandists have always known.

The biases, though, are also not only extrinsic. Humans have evolved a special ability to quickly discern the pertinent data in a large mass of information, and yet the shortcuts we take in our thinking also lead us to cognitive biases. That turns our evolutionary information-processing strength into a weakness, which we can only perceive with the help of others.

The complexity (from *com*, "together", and *plecto*, "to weave") of the world is greater than our individual ability to understand and process the personal and life-related challenges within it. When the challenges to be processed exceed our ability, we find ourselves at a critical juncture of education and learning. Almost every global crisis is of this nature. Sir Geoff Mulgan, Professor of Collective Intelligence, talks about social decision-making as a collective activity. What we need now is the ability to develop the process of bringing together our "shared brains", the mechanism of collective wisdom. We need a more functional, continuously developing communal process of human growth on the path to wisdom.

Surprises lie at the heart of such learning, which is about charting previously uncharted, unpredictable land – like conquering a rising incline. While we take over more of the unknown, we can also see further as we climb, and we come to realise that the unknown extends much further than we previously thought. Therefore, in climbing, we simultaneously increase both the conquered and the unconquered territory.

Old Language Stifles New Worlds

AT EARLIER critical junctures in history, humans have developed ways of easing problem-solving with the use of new, shared cognitive tools. Language and our ways of utilising it have led to pivotal steps forward. Language has allowed us to set and share common targets, and to formulate cultural concepts. The evolution of cultures accelerated significantly with the development of language. At the same time, humans improved their capacity for abstract and metaphorical thinking. The word metaphor comes from the words to carry over or transfer: metaphors are like bridges transferring meanings between two things that were not previously connected. Our languages are full of metaphors, some of which we use unconsciously: we don't really bear something in mind or catch someone's drift; our thoughts don't really race or form a train. Metaphors help us to describe things in ways that are easier for others to understand.

Literacy was a colossal step forward in the development of the human mind. The invention of writing and alphabets is a good example of how an innovation can spread far and wide when implemented in the simplest possible way. Similar shared tools have included myths, rituals, religions, music, mathematics, statistics and the scientific method. They are mechanisms we have developed for dealing with growing complexity at various points in the evolution of life in societies. They have helped us understand our shared reality, and to process and solve problems.

The main questions are, can we and do we use them in ways that benefit humanity? The internet, digital media and artificial intelligence are some of our newest collective tools. Unfortunately, we use them to fracture the cohesion within and between communities, and to increase conflict. The craftsman is losing control over his tools.

Professor John Vervaeke of the University of Toronto calls these tools psychotechnologies (Vervaeke, 2019). When new ones appear, they do not replace the old ones but rather add to them. Even though we no longer believe scientifically in the content of myths, they still have a lot to give us in the form of codified human wisdom.

Science gives us evidence that could tomorrow be disproved and replaced with better evidence: that is the self-correcting nature of the scientific process. Whether the latest data becomes the community's shared capital or not is a significantly more complex issue. Often, earlier truths that have already been refuted by sound evidence live on in a culture's persistent routines and beliefs.

As I mentioned before, the creation and development of words and language has been one of the greatest achievements of humankind. Language is a hallmark of perception: it tells us what we pay attention to, what matters to us, what our attitude to something is and from what perspective we view the world. Language has turned our individual hands into shared hands. Thanks to language, human creativity has been able to reach astronomic heights.

And yet, creating a word always implies taking something away from the thing that the word describes. Words are abstract and less than reality, and hence their usability – they are an easier way to process reality than reality itself. A map is not the same thing as the terrain, nor is a word the same as the thing it denotes. It cannot encompass the wealth contained in the thing itself, or comprehend the context in which the thing is situated. The more significant a concept is, the more closely we try to link its context into the words we use for it: hence northern peoples have more words for snow, and oenophiles have a whole vocabulary of descriptors for the qualities of wine.

Not everything can be put into words. Our indescribable feelings, perceptions, subtleties and nuances matter – sometimes even more than the describable things. Our fascination with controlling reality through words forgets the wordless side of reality because it is hard to express. This is why artistic, religious, romantic and humorous experiences are so hard to properly describe, but it doesn't make them less important, even though we tend to rate these inexpressible things less highly.

Words are instruments of control. They help us gain mastery over things. Verbalising a fear will shift focus to a particular thing and make us feel that we can master what worries us. That makes a specific fear easier to control than a vague anxiety that is not directed at a controllable source. We control words and thereby feel we control the thing itself. Life, however, is greater than words. We should be able to see the true nature of things behind the words. Hence the importance of using words deliberately and creatively, and the momentousness of experiences that render us speechless.

Just as virtual reality now feels like a threat against "real" reality, the creation of language must have felt like fearful removal from reality. Sceptics of virtual reality may identify with the deliberations of

Socrates and Plato on the relationship between spoken and written language. Socrates feared that written language would overpower face-to-face communication, which for him was the chosen tool of any lover of wisdom, i.e. philosopher. He emphasised internal self-knowledge as a source of wisdom and feared that writing, as an externally given factor, would weaken the power of our internal dialogue.

A word cuts a concept out of its context. Language created a new layer in our reality, but it has become reality to the extent that we forget that many concepts are simply shared contracts without a physical manifestation. We are unaware of the metaphorical bridges that stretch between reality and language.

In his book *Simulacra and Simulation* (1981), Jean Baudrillard describes us as living in hyperreality. By that he means a world in which the signs and symbols that we use, conditioned by modern media, no longer refer to the real world but to an intersubjective world of other signs and symbols. We are trapped in a self-replicating simulation of reality. A contemporary example of such a simulation are memes that we come across on our smart devices, which contain deep messages that we react to in milliseconds.

The soil of the information ecosystem largely determines the kinds of communal fruits and flowers that grow there. What responsibility does each of us have when it comes to the state of the information ecosystem? It is a common good, whose quality crucially affects our ability to understand reality and to formulate a shared foundation for handling the challenges of our time. The so-called tragedy of the commons also applies to the information ecosystem: when a resource is freely available to all, the benefits of selfish exploitation are enjoyed by a chosen few, but the drawbacks harm everyone equally. If no one shoulders the shared responsibility, the resource is crushed beneath selfish interests.

Often the meanings carried by language are valuable and crystallise a lot of collective wisdom. Our mother tongue and the thought structures it entails mould and condition our worldview. Do Finns have a different concept of equality because the Finnish language has no separate male and female pronouns, like many other languages, and only one ungendered pronoun (*hän*)? How is our concept of time affected by the fact that the Finnish language has no future tense and, instead, coming events are expressed in the present tense?

The influence of language is not always positive. When we come across something that conflicts with the mental models contained in our language, our inner voice tells us to distrust it and rely on our existing models. The more abstract the concept, the more likely our inner voice is to prevail. In some ways, our language returns us to factory settings when we try to find a new direction.

Writing about renewal is difficult because our existing language keeps us going down old paths. The deeper the mental models and beliefs being discussed, the more strongly they are linked to words, expressions and metaphors. That is something I have had to grapple with in writing this book. In describing tricky issues and systemic renewal, words such as 'solution', 'problem', 'game', 'build' or 'scalable' tend to pull us towards models that are inadequate for understanding the thing at hand. They are words from a linear and reductive worldview. When we want to change things, the words and the language used to describe that change must also evolve. It is not just a question of individual words, but of the whole way of understanding the world that is linked to them.

Precious Achievements Are Unreasonably Brittle

BUILDING DEMOCRACY and a functioning society is slow and demanding. It takes a lot of time to construct a complex system, alternating between specialisation and integration, continuously rising towards increasingly sophisticated capabilities and levels. Destruction, in turn, is quick. The rainforests of the Amazon can be decimated by logging or burning, while it takes forever (by human standards) for an ecosystem of that kind to be built up. Seeds may be preserved and the species that are spared from extinction may survive, but the recovery of a functioning ecosystem is a slow process.

Similarly, a democracy can be destroyed swiftly, but establishing the institutions that make it up and the trust that arises from their interaction is measured in decades rather than years. Complex systems usually have a degree of resilience arising from renewal, but if the system breaks down, rebuilding takes time. The exact point at which a liberal democracy ceases to exist is hard to define, and this is unfortunately being tested in many countries across the world.

Each of us has a specific perspective on reality. No one can see the whole picture. The angle from which we look affects what we see. The seer and the seen – the subject and the object – cannot be distinguished from each other, as they are mutually dependent. The rock garden of the Ryōan-ji Zen temple, a UNESCO World Heritage Site in Japan, contains 15 rocks. A maximum of 14 of them can be seen at any one time, regardless of the direction from which you view the garden. We can only ever see a part, never the whole.

To obtain a fuller view of reality, we need each other. Every perspective has some value. If we want a comprehensive picture of reality, we need to work together. Perceiving things from different perspectives, through the lenses afforded by different life experiences, is valuable for everyone. This is why cultural, ideological, religious and philosophical diversity is something to treasure. Communities with people from diverse backgrounds can produce better results together than homogeneous ones.

Just as two eyes view the world from slightly different positions, and the eyes seeing together give us the experience of depth, so specialisation and integration are both necessary, two mutually complementary processes. Specialisation receives its proper value from being integrated into a more extensive whole. For example, a child learning to read will first learn each letter separately. When the separate letters are understood as bigger wholes – syllables and then words – the secrets of language become unlocked. Once individual words are understood together as full sentences, entirely new worlds appear before our eyes. In this way, the child progresses from learning letters to understanding syllables and, with practice, reading fluently. By the time reading is automatic and subconscious, it has become a consolidated competence.

According to a theory presented by neuroscientists, what we learn becomes stored in our brains in a more generic and abstract form while we sleep. We connect what we have learnt to a broader context, an overall vision. At that point we no longer just know but *understand*, and what we have learned becomes a part of our identity.

Similarly we could consider the need for people's different views and mental models to complement each other. The aim is not for everyone to be of one mind, but for our differences to be synchronised harmoniously. In other words, diversity in itself is not enough; we also need a shared framework within which diversity can blossom. Maximal diversity is not an end in itself; it requires enabling limitations to bring diversity together in a way that benefits everyone. It is not a question of becoming homogeneous but of appreciating uniqueness, allowing for the uniqueness of others and building connections with what is shared.

Progress Casts a Long Shadow

I F YOU had been born two centuries ago, you would most probably not be able to read this, or any other text. Only one in ten persons globally born in 1800 learned to read. Your likelihood of dying before your fifth birthday would also have been 43 per cent (Our World in Data, n.d.). Today, it is 4.3 per cent, and illiteracy among children is below 10 per cent. That is progress. In many respects, decision-making, science and technology have led us to a higher quality of life and well-being. Still, I have tried to ask Google who it was that promised that the world would always and forever get better. Others have highlighted that belief in progress is one of our hidden thought patterns (Schmachtenberger, 2024).

In the early days of motoring, specifically in 1865, a Locomotive Act was passed in the UK. It decreed that horseless carriages – later known as cars – could travel at a maximum speed of 2 mph in cities. Additionally, they had to be preceded by a person walking at least 60 yards ahead, carrying a red flag. This may sound ridiculous now, but I believe that the lawmakers of the time were genuinely worried about excessive risks being taken.

The future has never been certain or predictable. For every generation, the changes that happen are exceptional compared to prior experience. When I held my first job in the Finnish Parliament in the late 1980s and early 1990s, the future and how to build it were something most political parties wanted to identify with. It stood for positive anticipation, the possibility of something new. Over the decades, I have seen the idea reverse from positive to negative. The future has become a threat, a possible disaster that we would like to escape from into the past. Political parties are afraid to become identified with the future.

An interesting and divisive point of our times is the question of whether we are doing better or worse than before. Many scientists and visionaries, such as Steven Pinker or Hans Rosling, will tell us the former: the number of people in abject poverty has fallen, as have illiteracy and child mortality, while the number of children in school has grown. Others, such as the authors Yuval Noah Harari or Margaret Atwood, see the future in a much bleaker light. In their view, humanity is about to destroy itself with the help of artificial intelligence and genetic manipulation, and nations are heading towards becoming class societies based on slavery.

My generation grew up wearing glasses tinted with the rose colour of our belief in progress. Every new generation was expected to live better than the one before. Currently we are in a cycle of negativity, and the crises of our internal and external worlds feed off each other. (The link *could* also work in the other direction: positive steps in mental health can lay the groundwork for positive decisions in our external reality. And if we give nature opportunities to recover from the destruction we have caused, we simultaneously promote the healing of our own minds and bodies.)

The idea of progress arises from an idealistic comparison between present and future. But are past, present and future even comparable in terms of progress? If we compare the years 1970 and 2020, has progress taken place? Is the arrow pointing up or down? It is like comparing an orange with a watermelon. Because the watermelon is bigger, you could say that progress has happened. The orange is a fine fruit, and a watermelon is lovely too, but their properties are entirely different. Are humans better off than before? Is the world more beautiful than before? Are we closer to the truth? Is climate change progress?

The problem with our focus on progress is that 'humanity' does not think or act. Humanity is not a cohesive agent that can act reasonably, and so we always act in ways that have both desirable and undesirable consequences. While solving earlier problems, we have generated new ones, and these are characterised by being global, quickly scalable and linked to the very future of humanity. Instead of stopping to measure suffering or well-being at different times with a tape measure, we might want to examine the processes we are caught up in and the contexts in which we now live.

I remember the threat of nuclear war from my childhood. Only the balance of terror prevented weapons of mass destruction from being used in that polarised world. Each of the competing alliances had a strong incentive not to deploy its arsenal. These days, the risks are not limited to nuclear weapons, as there are many ways of causing widespread destruction. The stakes are rising and the nuclear arms race logic is pervasive, with the distinction that there are no longer just two opposing players but many. Some of the players are anonymous and they possess cards that are unknown to the other players.

It is a curiosity of human cultural development that when we have successfully achieved something, the methods that wrought the success have started to permeate everything we do. The market economy, for example, has been an effective way to use competition to respond to people's needs, develop ever-better products, and allocate resources. We can thank the market economy for many welfare-enhancing innovations and making them available to the masses. At the same time, we have enabled the market to colonise areas where it is unsuitable. We have also turned its volume up so high that its short-term efficiency-seeking has become a long-term weakness for humanity.

Another example is our success in reinforcing specialisation and the division of labour in society. Many problems have been addressed by creating new disciplines, professions, and responsible organisations. However, this same idea has now been taken so far that solutions are developed in isolation and no longer form a coherent whole. They are insufficiently integrated to meet people's everyday needs – and what was once a solution has itself become the problem.

A critical task of the media is to bring diverse views to the public's attention so that in elections, citizens can choose between them according to their own values. In this age of competitiveness, however, this valuable tool can become a way of emphasising polarisation. Extremes get more visibility, and visibility means rewards in the attention economy, as well as votes. As a result, striving for truthfulness and finding shared solutions are the first victims, and democracy itself could be close behind.

All these are examples of important human problem-solving tools that would need renewal to work better. It is tempting to state that the tools are wrong and that it is time for the pendulum to swing to the other extreme in our 'either/or' binary thinking. That is not a sustainable solution. Instead of "no, but" we must learn to say "yes, and".

The ancient philosopher Heraclitus is seen as one of the fathers of the dialectic of opposites. Although he emphasised the fact that things are impossible to understand without also understanding their opposites, for him opposites were part of one and the same thing. Instead of making opposites an end in themselves, we must focus on understanding their mutual dependency. The tension-causing polarisation is defused and the problem dissolves, like individual raindrops as they hit a lake.

When we change how we look at the world, the world we are looking at changes, to paraphrase Max Planck. The ability to integrate things seen as opposites generates huge opportunities for innovation. As polarisation is defused, it can make space for advancing to a new level. It's time to move beyond polarisation – toward deeper complexity and a more integrated understanding of diverse views. Instead of creating opposites we must recognise that every perspective has its own story and uniqueness to offer in our collective learning.

The culture we have inherited – whose most beautiful and truthful products we have received from preceding generations – is our most important capital. Every word, concept and idea we learn is an achievement handed to us by earlier generations. This inheritance also involves the duty to pass the baton forward – not as it is, but improved, just like those who went before us tried to do.

We are living through an interim period in which too many attention-grabbing things cannot be left unattended, but we lack the understanding, language and sustainable model for a new setup. We subconsciously feel that something is missing, and are blindly bumping around looking for it – something deep and essential to humanity, which was once understood, but which has been bypassed by other achievements and forgotten over time. Do we know how to live? Are we familiar with the path to a meaningful life?

Recognising our fallibility does not mean giving up on determination or hope; on the contrary, it is a part of the experience of responsibility. We are an element both of the problem and of the solution under development – and the new problems that that will bring. I believe in a future created in the here and now, in positive thinking and in humanity. Striving for what is good, beautiful and true is a strong and important part of being human. The thirst for progress will not be quenched, but we can be more careful what we drink.

The Idea of Problems Is Problematic

Albert Einstein is quoted as saying that if he had an hour to solve a problem, he would spend fifty-five minutes thinking about the problem and five minutes considering solutions. The crucial thing is how we define the nature of a problem: that determines the set of potential solutions. If our understanding of the problem is incorrect, we will end up with a bunch of unviable suggestions for solutions.

However, sometimes the very word *problem* is problematic, because we are used to thinking of problems as having solutions. The word *problem* inevitably makes us think of a solution. Solutions, in turn, are understood as permanent and final "fixes" to problematic situations.

Life has a lot of problems for which solutions exist. If there is no food in the refrigerator, going shopping is a logical move. There is no point thinking outside the box or applying a Socratic dialogue to the problem of an empty fridge. The challenges considered in this book, however, have no ultimate, correct or permanent solutions. They have no start or – unfortunately – end dates.

Such quandaries are sometimes designated 'wicked problems', as opposed to tame, technical or tactical ones (Rittel & Webber, 1973). Wicked problems entail paradoxes, intersecting lines of mutual tensions or conflict, which refuse to be solved. Try to solve them permanently and you will likely generate new issues somewhere else. This is why one sustainable way to deal with them is for all those involved to carry the tension together and, optimally, find a way to benefit from it.

Some challenges are related to our way of looking at the world, and those cases may call for a change in perspective. Instead of focusing on a solution, it is perhaps better to aim somehow to live with the issue that appears problematic. That is not the same as just accepting the unsatisfactory situation; on the contrary, the approach invites us to react consciously and strongly to it by refocusing or reframing. But it is certainly worth giving up the expectation of finding an ultimate solution.

Our culture is thirsty for solutions. Humans have a tendency to draw conclusions even before a problem has been properly defined. Research has shown that if we don't find a solution to our perceived problem, our desire to move forward is so great that we'll go ahead and solve a different problem instead of the original one (Dunbar, 2017). We are also keen to solve other people's problems on their behalf, without listening to them or understanding their situations; meaning well, but producing poor results. This is why the sport of jumping to conclusions is not a healthy one to practise: the risk of jumping in the wrong direction is high.

Risks Are Agglomerating

ONE OF the biggest transformations taking place around us is a strong increase in mutual dependence. The simultaneous development of transport and communications together with growing wealth have led to a networked world, making it easy for people, ideas, goods and capital to move from place to place. Digitalisation has made location-independence and the mutual connectedness of data and operating systems even easier. Utmost interdependence makes it difficult to figure out the reasons behind things and to fathom cause-and-effect chains. Things are not found on a linear plane, but in a web-like fabric of multidirectional links, where everything affects everything else. It means that change progresses at an exponential rate, which is much harder to comprehend quickly.

Human comprehension has not naturally developed to operate in or cope with such an environment. Nassim Nicholas Taleb (2013) has given the name "black swan" to unpredictable and improbable "outlier" events. They are rare in the light of prior developments, but as they continually occur in our world, we have become better at dealing with them. Taleb has also popularised the concept of the "antifragile" – things or people that benefit from stress, variability, chaos and uncertainty. The term is related to resilience but goes beyond it by emphasising that many things can, in fact, benefit from disorder and pressure, just like lifting weights increases your muscle mass. This aspect has not been taken into consideration in our societies' processes. The ability of communities, societies and global decision-makers to integrate antifragile models into their cultures is the only sustainable way to anticipate coming situations.

It is not any single crisis or development chain we should worry about, but their combined and cumulative impact. In this respect, our risk management ability is lacking. We handle risks as discrete phenomena, rather than as cumulations of interdependent hazards. We have siloed individual risks by formulating separate scientific models and explanations for them, each with their own vocabularies, experts and professions dedicated to forecasting and preventing them. A risk is easier to control and less frightening if it is given a name and an owner.

The Covid-19 pandemic should have taught us that the original cause of the risk and all the things it affects cannot be individually controlled. Our current risks are intrinsically interdependent and culturally adaptive, with irremovable links to people's behaviour. The essential aspect of processing these risks is how they are defined. For example, climate change is simultaneously a biodiversity, democracy, food infrastructure, water, energy and physical and mental health problem. We have specialised in risk management and created hierarchies for working on it, but our integration ability is still vastly deficient.

Many of society's finest achievements, whether they be nuclear energy, electronic money or digital traffic management, simultaneously make up some of our most vulnerable risk agglomerations. When we solve problems, our solutions increase complexity, generate new issues, heighten risks and make us vulnerable to new crises and shocks.

The 2007/8 financial crisis was an example of how complex and innovative financial instruments could trigger an unforeseen avalanche. Our response to the crisis was to increase detailed regulation of the financial market, which, in turn, increased the complexity of the system. Seen in this light, the claim that "this will never happen again" seems less credible. Having recovered from the initial shockwave of the financial crisis, the OECD established their New Approaches to Economic Challenges (NAEC) initiative. It was based on the realisation that the organisation's inability to predict the crisis was due to having monitored the financial markets too narrowly, using only tools and foresight methods pertaining to economics. They now wanted to bring in a multidisciplinary approach, and to better understand human behaviour and motivation at the micro level. The work began enthusiastically, but the further back the financial crisis fell into memory, the further the initiative slid down the organisation's (and its member states') agenda.

The recent astronomical increase in information and disinformation makes it nearly impossible to form bigger pictures and to integrate knowledge. No one has a handle on the combined effects of diverse scientific innovations and technologies. Earlier industrial revolutions have been based on singular innovations that have allowed humans to harness a significant new resource. The Fourth Industrial Revolution differs from its predecessors. By definition, it is not caused by the development of an individual technology, but by the simultaneous maturation and integration of several technologies.

The question is, who understands the combined effects of these narrow areas of expertise, or the picture that they all form together? I feel that philosophy is reclaiming its importance as an essential subject in our time, returning to the role it once played among scientific disciplines: a research method that seeks to understand reality, knowledge, ethics, society and humanity comprehensively and by examining the practical applications of wisdom.

For example, we now inhabit technological environments where one mistake can lead to sweeping damage with immediate effect. Genetic engineering, lethal autonomous weapons systems and many artificial intelligence applications are examples of innovations with the potential for widespread devastation. If ninety-nine per cent of experiments with new technology are likely to go well but the remaining one per cent goes badly and leads to extensive damage, what should we do?

We stand before a novel kind of ethical responsibility, for several reasons. Our ability to modify reality, even humans themselves, down to our genes, indicates that we have received powers that mythology used to attribute to deities (Brand, 1968). The question now is whether we also possess the wisdom to use these powers in ethically sustainable ways.

Humans' instinctive self-preservation methods, which have been integrated into our heredity by evolution, protect us from many threats. We baulk at snakes and are nauseated by the smell of spoiled food. We have not evolved such reactions to climate change or biodiversity loss; rainforest destruction and ocean pollution don't generate a powerful feeling of fear, loathing or nausea. And yet, their impact on us as a species is just as serious as eating spoiled food or being bitten by a snake. Today's risks exceed our instinctive risk-management capacity. Invulnerability is a dangerous illusion, which makes us unable to prevent the snake from slithering into Eden.

In his book *Team of Teams: New Rules of Engagement for a Complex World*, General Stanley McChrystal writes about rigid and reductionist risk management. Describing the operations of US troops in Iraq in the early 2000s, McChrystal admits that the world's most highly funded, systematically trained and methodically led army units were unable to respond to the challenge posed by scattered, poorly resourced Al-Qaeda troops. The US Army's success in destroying Al-Qaeda leaders had led to the Islamist organisation developing operations based on agility, self-directedness and situation-specific reaction. What was perceived as a weakness had become a strength. Thanks to their ability to reallocate their limited resources in an agile manner, these troops eventually grew into the movement known as ISIS.

The World Economic Forum publishes an annual Global Risks Report. It is based on a survey that maps the probabilities and impacts of risks by asking respondents to rank a number of potential hazards. The published results profess to show what risks are considered the most likely. However, experiences of both World Wars, for example, indicate that it is not any single event or thing that causes risks to materialise, but the agglomeration of several mutually dependent risks in a specific moment.

Because war is a risk to be minimised, we must aim to unravel some of the agglomerations of risks that create the dangerous cocktail leading to the eruption of war. We also hear more and more predictions that the human race could go partly or wholly extinct in the next couple of centuries. And then we'll pour another cup of coffee and go on with our lives. The message must be causing anxiety, but the effect on our practical actions is usually small.

If we continue on this same path, the risk of a fateful end result is high. We should be able to step off the trodden path in a better direction. But how? It feels like driving on a windy mountain road in a car with a locked steering wheel: you can't steer and no one can unlock the wheel.

The facts are uncertain, people argue over values, the stakes are high and decisions are needed right away. Is it possible to continue operating in such a situation? Our first reaction is always to move the deadline, but we have been doing that for a long time now – too long.

I worry that we are exposed to grievous risk agglomerations. A dangerous cocktail is being brewed by the sum total of individual risks and the overwhelming nature of some of them. Earlier, risks would accumulate and erupt locally or regionally, and people in other areas would take heed and learn from the horror. Now the stakes are much higher: the wager is not a single region or country like before, but the entire planet and its ability to support life. There is no waiting until later to learn from others' experiences when we are all in the same boat. We are gambling and have bet the survival of our species.

Confusion Is Justified

HOPELESSNESS SPRINGS from a profound feeling of isolation, powerlessness to bring about positive change and inability to find meaning in one's own life. "The world is out there, and I can't do anything about it." "There is no place for me in this world." "I'm alone, and no one can understand the pain in my life." "I don't want to bring children into a world like this." "There is no point in living, I'm too tired to try." This could be a summary of the calls received by any youth support hotline in the world. The messages are characterised by a perceived disconnect between the self and the rest of the world.

The cultural reality we have created puts a strain on our mind's resilience. In 1979, the sociologist Aaron Antonovsky published the Sense of Coherence theory, according to which our perception of how manageable, understandable and meaningful our life is has a critical impact on our health and well-being. The phenomenon applies at the individual, community and societal levels. Feelings of life being unmanageable, unintelligible or meaningless are not good for anyone in the long run. Their effects reach into our mental and physical health alike.

When the world changes faster than the worldview to which we have become exposed, we become strangers. There is a clash between our understanding and our surroundings. We experience a culture shock, like that previously limited to physically travelling to another culture. In other words, we become estranged from the place that we believed to be most familiar. Our connections fade – with other people, with reality as we perceive it, with the meaning and management of life – and we lose the plot of our lives.

Have we created a reality that we ourselves cannot cope with? Some of the mental health challenges can likely be explained by the fact that we can now speak more freely about mental health than before, we have better mental health research, more accurate depression diagnoses, more prevalent pharmaceutical industry marketing. But is that the whole picture?

I worry most about the feelings of inadequacy, powerlessness and hopelessness experienced by young people, and the growth of mental health issues among them. This phenomenon, whose causes are hard to identify, tells us that something is badly wrong in our cultures. The change has taken place in a relatively short time, but stealthily, and has therefore appeared partly unnoticed.

We are exposed to a growing amount of information on everything that is worrying and disturbing in the world.

We feel that we lack the energy to care about everything. Caring is linked to agency – the ability to do something about a situation: homeless people on the streets, pollution in the seas, loneliness among the elderly, bullying in schools, growing national debt, a family member's sickness, the extinction of species. The desire to care turns into anger when we lack the time, the energy or the skill. Why can't someone else do something? Why don't the authorities, the decision-makers act? It's their duty after all! In the end, we become cynical and look the other way. We harden our hearts in order to cope. We disconnect from the world in which we live.

We are living in times of transformation and uncertainty. Fear and doubt feed off each other; in an uncertain reality, we are prone to be afraid, as if riding a ghost train without knowing that it is all fake. Uncertain times are also golden days for fearmongers. Increasingly, we are not feeling fear that is directed at a specific cause, but rather an unspecified, undirected anxiety.

In this state, our minds are not flexible enough to deal with surprises, and our capacity for self-reflection is limited. Our survival instincts of fight, flight or freeze come to the surface. If a significant proportion of people experience their lives in this way, humanity's ability to identify shared solutions is seriously impaired. The less we can influence change, the more likely we are to experience it as being external to ourselves. The less time we have to adapt to change, the more rigid, splintered and chaotic our society becomes. We become paralysed by trauma.

Having someone to blame is a relief. We use external threats to maintain internal cohesion – both as individuals and at the national level. That worldview consists of "us" and "them", winners and losers, zero-sum games, good and evil. Fear drives groups together like herds of antelope running from a lion. It is contagious. When it comes to people, the cohesion of a group is measured by the harmony of its members' opinions. When a community faces something frightening, it takes courage to have a differing opinion. Rulers, whose power relies on having an external enemy to fear, have always known this. Fear reduces our tolerance of diversity, narrows our minds and prevents us from seeing into the future. On the other hand, a differing opinion may free us from the paralysing effect of fear by bringing a new perspective into consideration.

Fear acts as a dam for more difficult feelings. In evolution, it has had to take other functions and emotions hostage to ensure our survival. Besides fear, though, hope is also an attitude for uncertain times. The two are like oil and vinegar: they don't mix. They cannot coexist, so one shuts the other out. A person who is full of hope is not afraid, while a fearful one often lacks hope.

Democracy cannot be based on fear; it must stand on reciprocal trust, which is one of the hallmarks of love. It is not about control but about taking a conscious risk that someone could break your trust. Reciprocity weaves the democratic system together through communal commitment. Fear, in turn, challenges democracy. In the field of world politics, a battle is being waged between fear and hope; each has its brokers.

An essential question for our time is how to temper our fear (or to fear wisely) instead of seeking to control everyone else out of fear. Climate change and worries over the survival of our species have raised collective fear to a new level, that of global trauma. The risk is that, in the long run, this fear will turn into cynicism, short-sightedness, contentiousness and narcissism. The alternative is to pass through fear to growth (as the saying goes), and to build novel approaches to mutually assured thriving on foundations of hope. Some of us are prepared to go ahead on our own, but together, supporting each other, we will get further. Hope is a security blanket to which we should cling.

Traumatic experiences can cause us to see events that surround us as manifestation of ill will: others are enemies, I am being persecuted, bad things always happen to me. Continuous exposure to threats and stress prevents us from learning. Events do not become integrated into a broader whole, nor proportioned to our life stories. We cannot see ourselves from a helicopter view.

One of the biggest societal changes of the last hundred years has been the dilution of the meaning of religion in our daily lives. Previously, religion was much more than a simple question of believing in a certain deity or higher power. Over the centuries, diverse significances and rituals that mattered to humans have been woven into them, and many of them comprise joint efforts to achieve collective wisdom and a good life. That is not to say that religions have only brought good things; history is proof of that. However, secularisation has also led to the loss of something valuable that has not been replaced with substitute rituals and traditions of inner spiritual growth. We are blind to the other elements that disappeared from our lives and which went hand in hand with religion.

Now each of us has to try separately to bring those elements back into our lives and identities from scratch. As a thought experiment, consider all the things that are actually included in an hour spent at church, temple or mosque: opportunities for quietening down, looking inwards, listening to ourselves, focusing calmly on what happens around us, feeling a sense of belonging with others, experiencing what it feels like to ask for help, to be forgiven and to forgive, being blessed, singing, being faced with and pondering the ultimate questions of life, being reminded of historical texts and thinkers, being connected with a millennial chain of traditions, asking for mercy, recognising our mistakes, seeing paintings or other artworks, being read aloud to, reciting texts with others, participating in ritual. This experience package is the result of thousands of years of development; similar elements are found in all of the world's great religions.

When these ritual contents are rejected on the basis that we do not believe in the supernatural or in a higher power, we lose a large variety of valuable things. No replacement for them has been developed; a weekend visit to a shopping mall won't fill the void. When everyone must create those dimensions, which are essential to our humanity, from zero in their own lives, it's no wonder we feel under pressure; no wonder we feel we have lost the meaning and purpose of life, the significance of the everyday.

As the significance of religions as value systems has weakened, the responsibility for our life choices lies ever more with ourselves, without an external bellwether. Yet, at the same time, this individualistic reality with a multiplicity of values makes it hard to discern any shared direction for a people.

A culture is like a car on autopilot: you follow its lead unless someone grabs the steering wheel. The more cohesive the culture, the stronger the autonomous driving – and the greater courage is needed for swerving off onto a different road. Unless you consciously and specifically decide what kind of parenting you subscribe to, what rooms are included in your home or what your circadian rhythms are, the culture will decide those for you.

It would be easier if the anxiety we felt could be blamed on a leader, an ideology, a technology or a religion. We find it more difficult that it is caused by a nameless, leaderless, unorganised network to which each of us is tied. Many of us will blame a variety of external bodies while feeling some guilt inside, but that is the best we can do with the methods that we have. We are alienated strangers, stuck in a situation from which we cannot extract ourselves.

The invisible power that flees from democracy finds its form in algorithms, medicalisation, finance capitalism, populism and racism. Must we simply accept that the outside world is changing in ways that we cannot affect or influence? We love to say that we each build our own futures, but what if the feeling that reality is just something that is happening to us is actually an astute analysis of our shifting world? What if, given our current circumstances, we lack the ability to harmonise our inner and outer realities? And what if our democratic leaders are just as confused as the rest of us about how and where the most meaningful decisions are made? What if frustration, alienation and cynicism really are the right response to what we are experiencing?

We Do Not Seem to Know How to Know

KNOWLEDGE HAS become a weapon. It is used against people and for pushing agendas. If one side wields such a weapon, the other side will respond in kind.

A sphere of knowledge has its own ways of organising information and determining what has significance. A sphere of knowledge fences certain pieces of information in and others out, designating what is seen as valuable – and what is *not seen as not valuable*. If a professor from an eminent university expresses an opinion on a matter within their area of expertise, we are likely to trust it and value it more highly for arising within the rules and framework of science and academia. Mathematics, natural history, social sciences, the arts, power hierarchies, religions and indigenous peoples' knowledge models are examples of diverse spheres of knowledge.

The bastions of our spheres of knowledge are now being demolished from the outside, while their natural internal development keeps them in motion. By nature, science reviews and rectifies not only its results but also its definition of itself. This important self-rectifying process is hampered in a situation where the justification of its very existence is questioned from the outside. Energy is spent on defence that should have been spent on internal renewal.

The challenge posed to earlier spheres of knowledge is linked to the shift from the asymmetric diffusion of worldviews (from one to many) to the more symmetrical state of individualistic concepts of reality for which the internet stands. This has been hardest to accept for the elite – the part of society that had climbed to the top of the hierarchy to represent expertise, whether it be in politics, the media, religion or academia. Suddenly, not everyone agrees on the "correct" opinions and truth.

Individualistic truths have brought us to an arena for discussion where opinions, beliefs and facts become hopelessly jumbled. People justify their views by saying "that is how I feel," "that is how I see things" or "that is what I consider to be fact." The authorities that used to rule in the background are now wreathed in mist. Different spheres of knowledge are utilised flexibly as needed and where appropriate. We now live in a world of numerous competing spheres of knowledge, and our swift, global information sharing is only intensifying the competition.

Is it not every person's own decision whether to log onto the internet or social media, and what to do once there? Yes: the first step is our own, but after that our second and third steps are conditioned by the environment. The platforms in question are designed to optimise how long you spend there, how likely you are to return and what the data about your consumption and other choices will be used for – without your knowledge. Influencing becomes strategic. Information is shared to make individuals behave and think in specific ways. We are utilised and moulded to become specific kinds of people, rather than growing or being allowed to grow into our true selves.

Social media destroys our ability to make sense of reality. The amount and level of competence that has been harnessed to achieve this is astounding. We receive social media services for free in exchange for gifting data on our behavioural models to advertisers and influencers. It is a global trade-off.

Social media developers have found our weak spot, our Achilles' heel. They make full use of this weakness because it brings them success and profit, so the development will not stop. Our desire for attention, our tendency to become addicted to positive feedback, or difficulty in controlling our will when meeting new impulses, and our need for belonging to a group are all harnessed to ensure that we spend as much time as possible on the internet and on social media.

Distrust and mistrust, fear and anger have been and continue to be important for human survival. We could not cope without them. They are reactions to potentially threatening external stimuli. Now they have been hijacked for other purposes: they are the oxen pulling a cart to earn money and power for someone. Technology should be used to help people overcome their weaknesses and to correct the biases in their thinking and comprehension, but instead we use it to reinforce and exploit weakness, heighten biases and cause dependency. It is the tail wagging the dog; the means dictating the ends.

One could say that humanity "grew up" when it developed into a less violent version of itself that could manage conflicts. Now that we have exposed ourselves to the growing pressures of the last decade, humanity appears to have regressed into adolescence.

The knowledge war isn't about persuading people to believe things they don't yet believe; it is about reinforcing their belief in things of which they already have an inkling, attaching fear and hatred to these things and then directing these emotions at the desired targets. In fact, it is not about knowledge or information at all, but about feelings and how to channel them. Like plants reach towards the sun, we humans are naturally sensitive to how others react to us. This characteristic of our species is used as fuel for conflict.

Our discussion culture has run away with us. We are made equal to our opinions, and those who disagree with us must be against us. Identity politics has reinforced this equation, making every differing opinion an attack against one's identity, selfhood and person. Opinions and facts become stuck together like overcooked spaghetti – a vague mass without definition. We berate those who disagree with us on social media and that gives us pleasure. Anyone who has been dragged out of their bubble into abuse from another bubble has felt it in their skin. We use feelings of shame, rage and disgust in our discussions. Calling people *idiots, racists, fascists* or *snowflakes* somehow raises us above them.

We seem to end up in an infinite loop of finger-pointing of victims and scapegoats. We victimise ourselves in order to blame others, somehow simultaneously being the crucifier and the person being crucified. The desire to crucify others by public verdict is a picture of today's neo-religiosity: our sins are pointed out but no redeemer is in sight.

Over the centuries, we have developed numerous safety features for the physical world: we keep our doors locked, the use and display of firearms and other weapons is restricted by law and our defence forces secure our territorial integrity. In the virtual world, the development of safety and security features is still in its infancy. Services that are focused on controlling our minds and attention, in particular, have no defence mechanisms. In fact, we welcome these intrusions with open arms. We have developed technology that facilitates communal interaction, but our ability to interact wisely is, thus far, fairly low.

We Fail to See Ourselves as Predators

PREDATORS AT the top of the food chain obtain their nourishment by preying on others, but they do so only to satisfy their needs. We humans differ from other species in this respect. Our ability to come up with new needs and to utilise anything possible for financial gain, with increasing efficiency, has led to the impression that we stand outside or above the food chain, separate from nature's mutual dependencies.

In nature, predator and prey live in symbiosis, not as individuals but as species in an ecosystem. They need each other. If predators eat all the prey, they will soon be left without food. If prey animals evade all predators, they will multiply uncontrollably and quickly use up their own food and habitat. Evolution ensures that predator and prey evolve hand in hand, thus ensuring the survival of both. The increase in speed of a cheetah's sprint leads to natural selection favouring the antelope that are either fastest or most skilled at evasion.

Man as a predator does not follow this logic. Through our cultural evolution, we have developed tools that place us in an asymmetric relationship with respect to other species. We can fish all the tuna out of the sea before the tuna have the time to evolve to outwit our fishing tools.

Our ability to exploit the environment, not just to feed ourselves but more and more effectively and at increasing scales, has led to an unsustainable situation. We modify the environment to suit our short-term interests. The consequences are climate change and biodiversity loss.

These, in turn, lead to secondary consequences: climate change is expected to render many regions unliveable, causing more people to be displaced than ever before in history. Tertiary consequences include the competition for sustainable living conditions, food and drinking water which will significantly increase the risk of conflicts and violence. These follow-on effects are not limited to the places where they originate; they will reach every corner of the world. It is not just a global sense of duty that calls us to prevent this process: it is greatly in our interests to do so.

Recognising and admitting facts is difficult for humans when things have been a certain way for a long time. It is difficult to understand that every community is global in nature these days. The well-worn term *globalisation* means that there is now a dense network of operators that covers the whole globe, to which we all belong.

The economy has been at the forefront of this globalising process. Having a global network of businesses is a relatively recent phenomenon, and global financial, production, logistics and communication structures have sprung up to support it. Joint decision-making has not evolved at the same rate, nor has the ability to take into account values and principles that will safeguard the well-being of people and the environment. Challenges such as those related to cyber security and cryptocurrencies prove that the digital reality does not recognise national boundaries. These issues involve many players besides governments, and sustainable codes of conduct can only be created at the global level.

Although global questions have an enormous impact on the economic development of nations and citizens alike, we go on living as if that were not the case. UN Secretary-General António Guterres has urged countries to declare a state of climate emergency, because as long as nations approach global challenges as a zero-sum game, no one will move forward with the necessary actions. The "us first" approach copied from one nation to the next unfortunately does not refer to "us" as the people of the world, including future generations, but to certain privileged parties over others. History is full of justifications as to why one people should benefit or be compensated more than another. It is only when the threat looming jointly over all of us is recognised – hopefully before the suffering is too great – that the conditions will be right for equitable, appropriate action that corresponds to the global reality. Until then, suffering will grow in the form of worsening living conditions, climate refugeeism and battles over drinking water, which will manifest themselves as conflicts between nations and other groups.

In the last two hundred years, individual ecosystems have been destroyed all around the world. Now, we have the power to destroy the whole planet's ecosystem. As a species, we have developed the ability to annihilate ourselves, as well as all life on Earth.

Never before have so many people had access to such means of destruction. From a world with a handful of nuclear powers, we have moved on to a plethora of chemical and biological weapons, whose manufacture does not require the backing of governments. Previously, the power to destroy was limited to a few hands. Now, individuals can access the materials for formulating widespread devastation. This can happen in secret, behind closed doors, which means that even multilateral agreements between governments cannot prevent it.

The worldview of economic globalisation and its inbuilt incentives are based on turning natural resources into financial value. Each shift in our progress from hunter-gatherers to farmers, then producers of replicable factory goods and eventually office workers has been about utilising natural resources in increasingly efficient and intensive ways. The progress has been accelerated by a competition, in which whoever can convert natural value most efficiently into financial value is the winner. Along the way, obtaining our daily bread has lost its significance in the developing world; earning money has become an end in itself, to which all the hierarchies and power exercises in society are linked.

When we harness natural spaces for our use, we destroy ecosystems that have evolved over millennia. Evolution has fine-tuned the specialisation of organisms in interaction with each other and integrated them into a shared environment. This means that ecosystems evolve slowly to become increasingly complex. The development of the Amazonian rainforests into the wellspring of diversity that they are today has taken forever from a human perspective, and yet they can be burnt down in a single day to turn into farmland. Even if one day we decided to rebuild the rainforest, we could not do it. Maintaining farmland requires continuous human activity. The resilience of the former ecosystem vanishes and is replaced by a vulnerable entity that is at the mercy of pests and temperature fluctuations. We build the environment to be dependent on ourselves, bolstering our image as lords of all we survey.

But why should those living in poverty in Brazil not have the right to clear forest into farmland, in order to make a living, just as humans have done everywhere in the world since the advent of agriculture? It is an important and valuable question. It crystallises the dilemma that as individuals, we do not fathom the permanent damage we have caused to the environment as a species, damage that threatens to become our doom. We are not aware of our global identity and the ethical responsibility that that entails. Unless we find better and fairer ways to collectively ensure the nutrition and welfare of the global population, future generations will have increasingly limited options upon which to build their lives.

The utilisation of natural resources has followed the logic of the arms race. Treaties have been in place to try to rein in resource use so that everyone could benefit in moderation, and the environment could have time for renewal in the long term. There have always been freeloaders, however, who have developed ever more efficient and intensive ways of ravaging the environment, and suddenly the arms race is in full flow. Awareness of the fact that everyone will eventually suffer if we privatise the benefits of the environment but socialise the damages arising from its use, has not prevented this progression. Until now there have always been new areas to conquer and new seas to fish, but we are coming to the limits of the Earth.

The human species is characterised by the ability to achieve targets we set for ourselves. When we take it upon ourselves to aim for something, we build our worldviews and morals to fit this aim and create incentives to support its achievement, doing our utmost to make it happen. We are getting what we have measured: a growth in GDP, but at the expense of environmental destruction. This is a problem. Our targets, worldviews and incentives have a built-in self-destructive power.

As a species, we are causing consequences that we, as individuals, do not want. Although communications cover our entire global reality, we are not cognizant of our power of destruction. We can't think about the mutual dependencies and systemic changes that the sum total of our individual actions is causing. The idea of collective wisdom, of making ethically sustainable decisions in each situation, is what we need right now; it could save us as a species. We need to reconcile different needs and opinions, using and valuing them in our progress, changing directions non-violently, and finding a path for the survival of the species that brings everyone together.

The increase in global mutual dependencies has made the world less and less predictable. A small shift can have enormous after-effects, both good and bad. When the temperature is close to zero, only a very tiny change in the ambient temperature is needed to cause freezing; similarly, striking a single match can cause a huge blaze if the environment is parched. The same is true in society, and it has repeatedly happened in history. The 19-year-old Gavrilo Princip carried out an assassination that sparked the First World War, which led to the deaths of 16 million people. The conditions were such that one action sent the world up in flames. Humanity has once again created flammable conditions, and it is not hard to imagine a single action igniting a global catastrophe.

As highlighted above, traditional risk management, whose aim is to define and minimise individual risks, cannot cope with the concept of systemic risk – the cumulation and overflow of secondary and tertiary consequences caused by complex, uncertain and ambivalent realities. Systemic risks are a question of real processes that surpass the boundaries of sectors and industries and progress in nonlinear and random fashion. So they are difficult to identify in advance. Our innate way of thinking as humans is not great at predicting systemic risks. For the same reason, it is difficult to develop legislation or other regulatory means of managing them.

These risks have existed at earlier times in history. The difference now is in the scale, replicability and speed of their impact: the risks affect the planet as a whole. In our interdependent world, our destructive power is no longer local but global. To find the path to a sustainable future, we must go back to the roots of our worldview.

We are like coastal flowers transplanted into the mountains.

Language has turned our individual hands into shared hands

Humanity appears to have regressed into adolescence.

The craftsman is losing control over his tools.

When the world changes faster than the worldview to which we have become exposed, we become strangers.

Democracy cannot be based on fear; it must stand on reciprocal trust, which is one of the hallmarks of love

Humanity is not a cohesive agent that can act reasonably.

Fear acts as a dam for more difficult feelings.

We are utilised and moulded to become specific kinds of people, rather than growing or being allowed to grow into our true selves

Perhaps the time for striving for a consistent, singular worldview is over.

The desire to care turns into anger when we lack the time, the energy or the skill.

The future is a foreign country

Part Two: Perception

Q: How do we reckon with the challenges we are facing?

A: We have to encounter the ideas we perceive with. We are overtrained and undereducated. We have to learn to see our own eyes.

1. *The Illusion of Simplicity*
2. *The Illusion of Control*
3. *The Illusion of Divisibility*
4. *The Illusion of Competition*
5. *The Illusion of Technocracy*
6. *The Illusion of Development*
7. *The Illusion of Anthropocentrism*
8. *The Illusion of Knowing*
9. *The Illusion of Relativism*
10. *The Illusion of Permanence*

At the age of seventeen, I set off for a year's exchange from a small town in rural Finland to the metropolis of El Paso, Texas. There, I followed the Rio Grande border river on a daily basis to go to my school, which was next to a Native American reservation. Opposite, on the Mexican side, was Juárez, whose homicide rate made it the most dangerous city in the world at the time. The exchange student handbook's description of culture shock was nothing compared to what I initially felt. The Mexican food burned my mouth, the blazing sun burned my skin, and homesickness burned my insides.

The junctures and conflicts between American, Mexican and Native American cultures, the mindsets, the concepts of time, the urban environment, the habits and routines were wildly beyond my worldview. Everything I had tried to understand about the world until then suddenly appeared in a different light. I could not communicate very well yet, especially as nearly everyone spoke Spanish outside of school. I was different from everyone – a stranger – and there was quite a storm inside my head. I yearned to get back to a place where I was understood and I understood others. I felt homesick not just for a physical location and its people, but also for a familiar worldview and a way of life. I would somehow have to synchronise the reality there – my living environment for the next twelve months – with my ways of thinking, or I would never survive.

I ended up finding the answer in music, specifically through joining the big band and marching band, where I felt instantly at home. The first time I attended rehearsal, a connection was created that helped things fall into place. I rediscovered the power of a shared language in music and its ways of communicating. I had been playing music for years, so orchestra stands, instruments, the interaction and the joy found in music were all familiar to me. I became an agent and the rehearsal rooms, my arena of action.

Being in tune with the rest of the band allowed me to fine-tune my concept of reality to the environment. The world became more cohesive. My inner self, and with it the homesickness, calmed down. I quite literally caught hold of the melody and eventually it turned out to be one of the best years of my life.

A similar phenomenon is at play in our anxiety at the changes going on in the world. Even those who do not travel stumble over conflicting experiences caused by the increase in volatility and unpredictability, and the diversification of the world's values. Our instruments are out of tune with the rest of the orchestra. A piano is out of tune when its strings are not vibrating at the correct frequency in relation to each other; pitch is always relative to something else. Just like an instrument, our worldview is not always in tune; our attitudes and perceptions do not always resonate at the same relative frequency to the external world.

A symphony orchestra will tune up before the start of a performance: an oboe gives the pitch and the others tune their instruments accordingly. We are living through a period of transformation, in which we are trying to retune our worldviews but cannot hear the correct pitch. We are still waiting for the clear and nasal tone of the oboe. The lack of a fundamental, shared tune causes anxiety. The scientific worldview is important, but it is not the one we live in daily; it was not designed for living.

Conflicts always exist between the mind and reality. In music, perfect harmony can be beautiful but tensions and dissonance can also enhance the melody. The same applies to life: tensions are opportunities for growth and learning. As we grow, we gradually learn to encounter and handle dissonance and to operate in the twilight zone between the known and unknown, the certain and uncertain.

Difficulties arise if the dissonance between our worldviews and the external reality is so extensive that it stops us from laying down our life paths, having agency and connecting with the community.

My contention is that we have narrowed our current worldview so much that it stops us from reaching our potential as humans. We are less than what we could be. Optimally, we can be present and united with our external reality in a way that generates powerful agency and meaning for our lives. The world's problems are not technological or mechanical, but the result of a skewed worldview and of illusions that blur the bigger picture, preventing us from seeing it.

Why do I call these phenomena illusions? An illusion is an unreal impression of something real, distorted by our senses. It is not that the things we perceive are non-existent or deliberate *delusions*, but that something has a distorting effect on the big picture.

Our mental models create the framework for what we do and see. When we look at the world through that framework for long enough, we cannot imagine anything outside of its boundaries. Our mental models become anchored in actions, and turn into mechanical, automatic routines. There are many such phenomena in our time. They weaken our ability to understand and take meaningful action. An illusion might not apply to the whole of reality, but it is so strong and impactful that it impairs our interpretation of the whole.

We have a dualistic worldview in which one must choose absolutely between reason and emotion, nature and nurture, masculine and feminine, heaven and earth, mind and body, good and bad, right and wrong, pretty and ugly, and so on, and this distorts our ways of understanding the world. Every day we are faced with situations requiring an either/or choice. Reading the news, we subconsciously ponder who is the villain and who is the hero of the piece. We make our choice, as we have always done and will continue to do, relying on the story's arc and archetypes and believing that there is a right answer.

While our pictures of reality have become diversified and segregated, people still hold certain widespread deep beliefs. We may not be aware of them or able to verbalise them, but they deeply affect our perception and our thinking about that perception: What is fact and what is an opinion? What are our values? Is human nature selfish or altruistic? How do we tell right from wrong? How do we make decisions? These are some of the core questions of humanity, but we approach them as most ordinary car buyers approach the engine: I don't care *how* it works, as long as it does. Why examine our deep beliefs if everything is going smoothly? That is a fair question. The answer is that better thinking leads to better living.

There should be more discourse on the roots of our thinking and deep beliefs. Unconscious though they are, they involve locks that can stop us from moving forward. Dualisms often involve hierarchies, by which one of the things in the balance is seen to outweigh the other. If we are unaware of these locks and hierarchies, we will be unable to process or utilise them in our personal growth. We should not be forming either/or settings but trying to observe a broader, more diverse and more balanced picture.

Some have said that the rise of postmodern thinking was based on our inability to move past the conflicts of dualism. It was easier to say that no truth exists, that everything is relative, than to try to find the source of the dualism. The postmodern tolerance of diversity of opinions does defuse some confrontations, but it simultaneously creates a new wall against people less tolerant of diversity. Suddenly, the relativity of opinions and values becomes the only truth.

It may be that we strive towards balance – a state where perfect harmony prevails. But the world around us does not favour that. It is continuously changing, living, generating new life, pulsating. The cycles of life are easy to discern in the progression of the seasons; in the germination and withering of plants; in how humans become fatigued and must rest to re-energise; in the heterogeneity of our civilisation and the tensions that follow. There is no centre of balance in the middle of a dualistic worldview. Any attempt to find one is doomed to fail.

Balance can be found in living with continuous imbalance, adjusting to changing reality and consciously maintaining tension. We cannot ultimately remove the tension that arises between the ideals of equality and respecting human diversity. Therefore, we need continuous discussion of how both of these valuable approaches can coexist. Optimally, we can make use of the tensions pulling in two directions at once. It can lead to something beautiful, just like a guitar string that cannot be played until it is tightened at both ends to create the optimal vibrations and sound waves.

"Path dependence" is a phenomenon that keeps us chained to well-established, familiar ways of doing things. It is like an addiction to gambling or smoking, in that we might know how harmful it is, and possess the will to stop, but the dependence prevents us from making changes.

Path dependence refers to well-trodden paths or ruts in which we can easily get stuck unless we consciously decide otherwise. The familiar path feels safe and secure. As the environment changes, however, it may lead us the wrong way. We may end up in situations from which we cannot extract ourselves. The system freezes and the path permanently enslaves us. Staying in our ruts, we will not encounter meaningful issues from which we can learn.

I am familiar with this situation, for instance from investigating inequality between schools in various countries. When a country ends up with a network of better and worse schools, it becomes nearly impossible to dismantle. I know several education ministers who are doing their all to achieve a more equitable system of comprehensive schooling in their countries. Their action plans always come up against a reality that upholds the division. The best schools attract the best teachers, the highest resources, the most important projects and the pupils from the backgrounds that are likely to give them better starting points for learning. The inverse is true for the lowest-ranked schools. Parents don't want the better schools to be shut down; they contain the promise of a better future for their children, which they are not willing to relinquish.

Our worldviews include incentives whose significance should not be underestimated. Incentives are important because they motivate us to either stay on our paths or set off on a new one. Illusions are a kind of subconscious incentive that directs us or encourages us to stay put. Illusions can be thought of as everyday 'truths' that direct our daily decision-making. We form our worldviews as part of our personal growth, and they fuse into the tacit knowledge that we rely on from the moment we open our eyes in the morning. These everyday truths of our various lived experiences are particularly important because solving the global problems linked to human behaviour implies participation from everyone.

If the solutions could be found by theorists or political decision-makers, it would be enough to ensure that their worldviews and realities are in tune. We no longer live in a world in which the views of men of the cloth or men of science – or any other men alone – are seen to provide a sufficiently comprehensive picture of the world. Over the centuries, we have broken our links with our bodies and souls, with nature, with the supernatural, with free will, with the meaning of life and with tradition. We are alone with our reasoning, and thereby often stuck. Making sure a few individuals' worldviews are in tune is not enough. Everyone's worldviews should be able to play their own tunes in a harmony that creates a better reality, and therefore it is necessary for us to look more closely at the illusions involved in our worldviews.

As someone who has suffered from poor eyesight since childhood, for me illusions are like lenses through which we see the world. Sometimes it is worth taking off our glasses to check how dirty they are. At the same time, we should also consider whether the prescription is still correct for viewing reality, or is it time to get a new pair.

The Illusion of Simplicity

THE BIGGEST conflicts between our worldviews and reality arise when we see the world as a clockwork mechanism, which, although complicated, is a closed system that works according to a regular logic. Something inside a clock may become worn or broken, but a professional clockmaker can open the casing, remove the broken part and replace it with a new one to make it work again.

One of the crucial characteristics of a clock is its predictability, which allows it to remain accurate. The interaction between the parts of its mechanism does not change but remains forever constant. We can rely on a clock working in the same way today as a year from now, always showing the right time. This mechanical worldview distorts how we see the logic of interaction between individuals and between communities. We expect to be able to predict how it will all work in a year's time. We are confident that an external expert will be able to fix any problem that arises in our community, and we imagine that as long as we set a strategy and allocate a budget for it, in a year's time things will have happened accordingly.

Difficulties arise when we apply the logic of a linear, closed mechanism to the wrong things. If a nasty case of bullying becomes public and causes a stir, politicians, feeling pressured, might decide to increase the number of school police officers, to implement new anti-bullying strategies in schools or to tighten disciplinary actions. The decision-makers see themselves as external experts who know the right answer and can reorganise the elements in the problem in order to solve it: the clockmaker opening the casing, identifying the broken part and fixing it. Their actions may be valuable in themselves, but they address the symptoms rather than the root cause. Therefore, they do not fix the underlying issue or guarantee that bullying will never happen again. The papers will be filled with people wondering why politicians can't solve the bullying issue once and for all.

The financial system is an example of a mechanical approach. Even its vocabulary is indicative. We make *corrections* if the *wheels* of the economy stop turning; we *rein in* or *spur on* consumption as if driving a horse-drawn carriage; we carry out *balancing measures*, as if perfect symmetry on weighing scales were even possible to achieve. Monetary policy can be *tightened* or *loosened* like nuts and bolts. These are tools handled by the fiscal policy elite, who know the quirks and tricks of the machinery and have complete control of the related vocabulary, way beyond the understanding of laypeople. Economic policy rises above everything, even politics; its clockwork turns the hands and lawmakers and citizens had better not interfere.

A simple structure allows for a continuum of clear causes and effects. Complex systems are set apart by the fact that they involve a living, growing element. We human beings are complex systems in ourselves, just like human communities and nature's ecosystems. In complex systems, the whole is more than the sum of its parts. Any changes in the parts permanently alter the operation of the whole. How the parts interact is more important for the functionality of the whole than how they work separately. For example, lungs are quite worthless unless connected to the vascular system that transports oxygen to the body's cells. It only takes a tiny change in the parts' interaction to have a huge impact on the whole. Look at your phone for a couple of seconds too long and cause a multiple-vehicle collision on a main artery into the city during rush hour, and it could lead to significant impacts on the whole city's logistics chain and a very bad day for many businesses and families.

Complexity has various dimensions, and here I would like to mention four that are most familiar to me.

Compositional complexity is simply that numerous factors act together to create an outcome. An example is well-being. The International Institute for Applied Systems Analysis (IIASA) has mapped national well-being systems based on research data collected by the OECD. Its results demonstrate the networked and multifaceted nature of the phenomenon, with its numerous feedback loops and interactions of various intensities.

Experiential complexity: Different people perceive the different dimensions of the same experience according to what is meaningful for them. Some people pay more attention to material conditions than to spiritual ones. Because the way in which we understand well-being is highly relative, the well-being level of others affects how we see our own. This is why the idea of producing or measuring well-being for everyone using the same means may sound fair but might not lead to the desired results.

Dynamic complexity is about the factors behind phenomena, their mutual interactions and how different people perceive the different factors change continuously and unpredictably. Social phenomena and their systems of interaction cannot be properly understood out of context and their contexts are always changing. Any detailed verbal description of a social system is almost certainly out of date. Similarly, no part of the system may be detached from the whole to be "fixed", because the functionality of the part depends on the broader whole. Remote work in the post-pandemic era has prompted very different reactions to the lack of physical contact with colleagues. Workplaces have had to come up with completely new forms of leadership and maintaining team spirit to cope with the dynamic complexity of the time.

Governance complexity is about recognising that in social systems, producing the desired results is impossible for anyone alone. No individual agent stands beyond the system's networks of interaction; each of them affects the system's dynamics with their actions. Having very specific delegation of tasks and reductionist targets, indicators and reporting models does not recognise the complexity of governance.

It is fashionable these days to talk about a need for systemic change. I fear the term is too often used without being understood. A system is not an external, technical structure that is separate from the people talking about it: achieving systemic change also requires renewal from the speakers themselves.

What is a system? Even the word has multiple dimensions. It is usually used to signify a mechanical system, such as a computer program or a society's hierarchical structure. These are examples of closed systems. Systems involving humans and other living things are open.

A complex open system has three main properties:

First, its openness means that it is exposed to flows and influences from the outside, which gives the complex system an always unfinished, emerging quality. The system shifts constantly, interacting with its surroundings, adapting to new circumstances. The parts of the system may only be analysed in relation to the broader whole. Second, because of its permeable boundaries, an open system is not constrained by a rigid and unchanging set of rules. It is for this reason that it is capable of descending into chaos. Third, it is nonlinear. Understanding chains of cause and effect in a complex system is challenging. A complex system consists of interdependent parts that together have greater capability than the sum of these parts, due to their emergent properties.

Systems aren't *out there* somewhere. A system is simultaneously a broad, abstract concept and a highly personal, nearby thing. Systemic change doesn't mean other, faraway people and things changing; it means you and me being a part of the changes we want to bring about. We have to change for the system to change.

We often confuse *complex* with *complicated*. The aforementioned clockwork is an example of *complicated*. In a complex system, the parts are mutually dependent. Because any changes in the parts and their interaction ripple to the whole system, developments in the system are difficult to predict, let alone plan. There is no external body that can modify the system as desired: the modifier always forms part of the system and its web of interactions.

We are ill-equipped to fully understand the nature of a complex system. Our collective decision-making, in particular, is a poor match for the complexity of our situations. We expect there to be a causal relationship between actions and consequences: you dig a small ditch with a spade and a large one with a digger. It is a characteristic of complex systems that this logic does not always apply. Small actions can have huge impacts.

Management consultant and complexity scientist Dave Snowden's Cynefin framework helps to make fuller sense of the range of situations inherent in understanding the idea of 'system' (Snowden & Boone, 2007). His quadrant model helps to identify contexts that are clear, complicated, complex and chaotic. When a context is *Clear* (known) things happen in a logical and linear fashion, cause and effect follow each other and the truth is known. Best practices are useful models and all that remains is to identify them. Each person is responsible for their own sphere and they have no reason to mess with anyone else's. When a situation is *Complicated* it is still in principle knowable but it will involve more options than just one linear, unchanging path. Here, we must choose between alternatives and make necessary changes, but the best experts can usually find the right solutions. However, when a situation is *Complex*, causal relationships are far from clear. Due to strong mutual dependencies between causes and effects, external influences often have a greater impact on, for instance, a person or an organisation, than their own actions. Leadership then consists of pointing self-directed individuals in the right strategic direction. Prediction is unreliable, so experimentation – often several at the same time – is a good way to learn about the nature and status of the system. The final of the four states, *Chaos*, is characterised by a high level of unpredictability, the absence of control and an all-encompassing ethos of survival. There is no time to know, investigate or experiment: you just have to act to stay alive. Survival instincts take over. Armies train for these scenarios.

All four situations may be true at once in different areas. *If* we can agree on what the current operating environment is like, the next challenging question is whether our operating models, cultures and organisational structures are consistent with this assessment.

Most of today's basic social structures, institutions and models of organisation, governance and action were built for a "known" world. Having spent several decades working for and in the Finnish Government, I can say that the operating environment has evolved from "clear" towards "complicated" and "complex". I contend that a large part of the reality of decision-making is currently taking place in a complex environment.

The models and tools we use may be high quality but they are no longer applicable to the challenges we face; this leads us to managing and organising things badly, taking incorrect action and having an inaccurate understanding of information flows. I believe that that chasm is the main reason it has seemed so hard, in recent years, to get decisions made and, especially, to have changes implemented.

The operating cultures of "complex" environments mean that the leader cannot determine what will happen and can only use the organisation's mission to point people in the approximate direction. After that, through experimentation and learning in a continuously changing context, they reinforce the organisation's ability to connect with and adapt to change.

We complain about the speed of change, but the root of our consternation is actually a question of a more extensive alteration in the nature of our operating environment. The concept of speed is much too one-dimensional for understanding this change; it is like describing falling snow by describing only the speed of the descending flakes. What makes snowfall so fascinating is actually the number of crystals, their size and density, and the way they dance with the air as they come down. Similarly, the change in a complex system consists of a multiplicity of variables, which can vary in quantity, specificity, intensity of change, forms of interaction and mutual dependence. We should learn to see the variety of the change and the dynamic nature of the variety, instead of just lamenting the speed of change.

Where does complexity spring from? It is the result of our way of solving problems. As we humans have shifted from being hunter-gatherers to agriculture, from trading food to having a financial economy, and from small shops to centralised retail and logistics systems, in the densely populated areas we call cities, every person and organisation in the resulting whole has become interdependent. We have formed a complex open social system. The historians J. R. McNeill and William McNeill (2005) skilfully describe this development through human history in their book *The Human Web*.

The challenges in a complex system also differ in nature from those in a clear operating environment. If there is extensive unanimity concerning the solutions to problems, and the outcomes of these solutions are known to a high probability, the problems can be called "tame". If there is broad disagreement on the solutions and the outcomes can only be guessed at, the problems are "wicked". It is pointless trying to solve them using the same methods as tame problems. Wicked problems have no solutions. They do not begin on specific dates or end when we want them to. They have built-in paradoxes: contradictory statements characterised by mutual tension. There are no pre-made solutions or recipes that can be followed to solve them. Wicked problems such as climate change, with their complex nature, lead to despair in a linear mind. We must evolve beyond this. Complex environments demand complex cognitive abilities.

If you try to solve a wicked problem from a single perspective, you are likely to create much bigger problems. Solutions must be enabled from within the problems' own context; this makes them unique and culture-specific, and they are the link between decision-making and execution. A large proportion of the challenges in our society are of this kind. The "problem–solution approach" is a significant error of judgement in today's operating environment.

Instead of pre-planning the future, the best way to prepare is to understand the present moment and the nature of the environment in which we operate right now. Understanding the context allows us to react and adapt to change. It is not a question of passive adaptation but of living with change. It is particularly important to discern the new opportunities that arise and that can be seized at each time.

A complex system can best be understood by relating to nature. The chains of events that happen in nature teach us the essence of the organic development of human communities. The coronavirus taught us a lesson we never asked for: we were able to observe the adaptation of the virus in its interaction with vaccines and human resistance. In developing new variants, it always finds more opportunities as the context evolves.

When we connect with nature, beyond the names and abstract scientific descriptions that we bestow upon it, we discern the limitations of our observation and perception and can gradually understand the character of complex systems. Their phenomena cannot be permanently solved as problems; it is wiser to approach the constantly regenerating nature of life in a way that respects and upholds it. We humans are not external observers but interacting agents in nature's open system.

As our civilization has developed, our livelihoods and survival have become less dependent on having a direct connection with nature. At the same time, our ability to understand and respect nature's complex systems has weakened.

My grandparents recognised twelve seasons of the year, because their profession and livelihood depended on them. It was evident that the fruits of nature would be beyond their reach if they did not understand the effects of weather, rain and temperature on the lives and growth of animals and plants. They needed to know the exact moments to start fishing perch and burbot, when it was still safe to travel over the ice, when the mushrooms were ready to be picked, and when to plant grain so that the frost does not destroy the crop. Their knowledge also generated an appreciation of and respect for the forces of nature.

Now our survival depends on what will happen to the ecological niche we occupy as a species – i.e. Planet Earth. It makes one wonder what kind of awareness and identity is required of us in order to keep our niche in liveable condition. Part of the answer is surely a global awareness and identity. Without it, we are doomed to systemic blindness, and humanity will have effects that none of us, as individuals, would want.

There seems to be a growing desire to drag our concept of reality back into a mechanical box that could be more easily controlled from outside or from above. People's yearning for strong leaders and nostalgia for the "good old days" with simple and punchy solutions feeds off this.

Complex is a tricky word, often with negative connotations. No one wants a complex maternal relationship, for example. The opposite of complex is not *simple* but *reductive*. The good thing about a complex is that it resists reductionism in its interdependence, giving rise to a bigger picture. Maximum complexity is not an end in itself, but the complexity of our thinking should match that of the environment. As our surroundings increase in complexity, so should our understanding and reasoning. Some cognitive scientists consider that human awareness developed in the first place to better respond to the diversification of living conditions (Corballis, 2012). Complexity may have acted as a way to work through complicatedness to reach a higher level of understanding, consciousness and awareness. Futures researchers tell us that this volatile, uncertain era is here to stay. It is a complex reality in which we must learn to exist.

The Illusion of Control

THERE IS an old anecdote about God and the Devil walking down a road, when God picks something up and puts it in his pocket. The Devil asks what it is and God answers, "Truth." The Devil says, "Give it to me, I'll organise it."

Organisation is humans' way of gaining control over things. If something is disorganised, we must organise it; nothing can be left to chance. We have always found reasons to eliminate randomness. Our ancestors explained away chance as something supernatural, which, interestingly, made it more natural to them. Any improbable coincidence was seen as a sign of something: good or bad fortune directed by fate, steered by the gods or other higher powers or written in the stars. Our scientific worldview has negated these explanations. When we get stuck on the idea of control, we close our eyes to a part of reality. We should be utterly stunned if things happen just as we had planned them: that is the real coincidence.

The idea of control can easily lead to every bad occurrence being viewed as someone's fault. We want our world to be just.

If we experience loss, it is an injustice that must have been caused by someone. It must be redressed. A family member dies? It's the doctors' fault. Divorce? Impossible spouse. Child performing badly at school? Lousy teachers. Having to tighten the purse strings? Immigrants are taking it all. We love to lay blame; it raises us out of helplessness back into control. Digging out a scapegoat and demanding retribution turns us into gamers, despots, narcissistic makers of demands.

How can we lead good lives if the world is not predictable or organisable in ways that allow us to lay down our paths? We love to tell young school-leavers to set five-year goals, make plans and work hard to achieve them. It is a widely shared recipe for success. It is good to be focused and decisive; it is also good to be open to randomness and life's whims. We have to be able to shift our plans when things don't progress as we had thought. It is important to be aware that sticking to our plans may limit our ability to find a meaningful life path. Plans are needed so that they can be changed.

What if we had the courage to look chance in the eye? Then we would understand why fortune actually favours the prepared. We should be open to chance – give chance a chance, as it were. Coincidence may bring very interesting offers. Perhaps life could feel a little less stressful and demanding if everything weren't in our own hands. The character Too-Ticky from the Moomins shows us the way: "All things are so very uncertain. And that's exactly what makes me feel reassured."

We have been taught to believe that reality is that which is measurable. Leadership of organisations is based on setting strategic objectives and measuring results. Rarely can all the desired outcomes be measured. If evaluations of success, progress in careers and rewards for performance are linked to measurable results, these are overemphasised compared to the unmeasurable.

Reality becomes distorted. True impacts often come to light slowly and are hard to measure, which means we end up measuring small outputs in the system. Reality is distorted even more. We build a jail out of truth, whose room for movement is continuously shrinking.

"Surely people like this can't exist!" I can vividly remember that phrase from fifteen years ago, as we stood around flipcharts at the headquarters of the Finnish Broadcasting Company (YLE). The company's programme developers had long been utilising quantitative data on what Finns were like and what they expected out of media content. Now, they had decided to look at actual people's real lives and lifestyles, instead of averages. They were amazed. Real people did not correspond to statistics or averages and refused to stay within their stereotyped boxes.

In his book *The End of Average*, Todd Rose describes how in 1950, the US Air Force measured 140 physical dimensions – including thumb length and the distance between eyes and ears – of more than 4000 pilots. The aim was to optimise the size of their planes' cockpits based on the resulting average measurements. But when they compared the averages to each of the 4063 pilots' individual measurements, they were shocked to find that not a single one of them was perfectly average (Rose, 2016).

The "law of large numbers", i.e the idea that multiple measurements reduce error, comes from the sciences. With large quantities of data, the margin of error diminishes and the result is calibrated to be closer to the truth. The same logic is sometimes applied to humans: we think that while everyone has small faults and anomalies, when everyone is put together and averaged, it will result in a perfect, true, "genuine" person. A person with an average of one testicle!

People are easier to deal with in the form of numerical data and we are often led by the nose by our averages. But humanity is characterised by uniqueness. By focusing on averages we fail to see each person's singularity. Those who can combine doing what they love with making use of their individual peculiarities have found something of life's essence.

The more we try to control things, the more the things start controlling us. Try to control the water by grabbing hold of it while you swim, and you will sink. Learn instead to trust the water and its carrying ability, and you may float on the surface. Similarly, if we try to control every unexpected event when faced with uncertainty, we will drown in them. We must learn to trust in our ability to live safely in an uncertain and unpredictable reality. Uncertainty will give us the dimensions of freedom that allow us to redefine our identities. Total certainty is a tyranny; uncertainty brings opportunity.

Because we love control, we fail to realise that we have ended up tightly wrapped in a tangle of individual issues and objects, like flies in a spider's web. We react to the objects of our control but forget to live our own lives.

Control is also a sales point: countless examples of the "sledgehammer" kinds of solution can be found in politics, consulting, health and lifestyle services and many more. US president Donald Trump is one of the most hardened representatives of this approach: some of his straightforward solutions, from building a wall to saving jobs by tariffs, have been highly popular. It would be great if such simple solutions worked. Usually, they just make the situation worse.

Smartphones are sometimes described as reality carried in our pockets. They really do bring the world and its events into constant contact with our skin. The opportunities afforded to us by communications, the internet and social media to be networked with the world make us feel that the world is just one click away.

It also gives us the illusion of being able to control the world with one click. We have numerous smartphone apps related to control in the form of measurable data, whether they be related to daily steps, maps or stock prices. This swiftly spreading consumer technology has managed to respond to a significant demand: smart devices are an answer to our need for control.

Many of our worldviews are based on the intuitive belief in the existence of an ultimate solution. It might be a scientific truth that will soon be revealed to us by scientists; perhaps a technological breakthrough that solves all our problems; or religious salvation, which will change everything. It might be an apocalyptic dystopia, or death and the end of consciousness. We await this resolution. Instead, could we see reality as more of a process characterised by continuity and openness without an end point? It might free us from waiting and allow us to take action here and now.

A good example of the attraction of control is the attitude that political decision-makers often have towards research and innovation funding. They know that a strong foundation of basic research is a prerequisite for the accumulation of competence and data needed by applied research. But once they have to choose between funding product development and applied research, it suddenly becomes very difficult to defend basic research before politicians. They think that by funding the research that is as close as possible to the birth of innovation, they can minimise the risks of funding. At the same time, however, they minimise the possibilities for coming up with genuine big innovations. When it comes to basic research, you can never really know in advance what findings, new data and evidence will emerge, and that is why decision-makers find it hard to commit to funding it. The pleasure of control makes applied research weigh more in the balance. The less certain and predictable the world becomes, the more we will need exploratory research – and yet, for that same reason, politicians in their yearning for certainty will take the opposite action.

Our deep-seated aspiration to be right prevents us from seeing the flaws in our reasoning. This attitude is detrimental to us, both as individuals and as a society. It makes us see those who think or act differently as ignorant and stupid, in need of correction. A belief in knowing the right answer stops us from seeing the multiplicity of alternatives that lie in store. Growth comes from ignorance, from curiosity and wonder before the unknown.

The Illusion of Divisibility

AROUND A century ago, a man called Frederick Taylor revolutionised the workplace. Observing the methods of factory workers, he noticed them working like artisans – each in their own ways, according to their own habits. If the manufacturing of pig iron by a large number of people was to be efficient, the work model must be simplified by limiting each individual worker's level of freedom. Artisanship was eliminated and factory work became standardised. For the system to operate effectively, instructions and messages must be clear and few. It was the foreman's duty to set the pace and keep things simple, and the factory whistle would keep time to the minute, to ensure a homogeneous and standardised process.

Taylor improved the efficiency of American factories by defining and subdividing work in terms of specific tasks, clocking each stage until it was optimal. He deserves some of the glory for the flourishing of industry in the United States, and his ideas were enthusiastically absorbed around the world. One of Taylor's central ideas was that processes must be subdivided and described so minutely that anybody is capable of completing them: 'One of the very first requirements for a man who is fit to handle pig iron as a regular occupation is that he shall be so stupid and so phlegmatic that he more nearly resembles in his mental make-up the ox than any other type.' (Taylor, 1911) The main thing was to separate labour from thinking; thinking and planning befell the management. Workers, in turn, must follow predetermined job descriptions to fulfil the plans, and never think. Any extraneous stimulus, even chatting with other workers, jeopardised control over the process.

The workers were good at following orders; the process worked and generated wealth, even though working conditions were questionable and the pace was set mechanically. In his day, Taylor did improve many people's quality of life: he made it possible for unskilled people who had just moved into the city to make a living. He was convinced that his theory was a blessing even for workplaces outside of the factory environment, such as public administration, and non-governmental and service organisations.

The labour market has long continued on the path laid by Taylor. Even though we might scoff at his quotations today, we still believe that it is the management's role to develop plans that are then subdivided and rolled out to lower levels of the organisation for execution. Have you ever felt forced to do silly things at work? that you do things you would never do in your own life? that you spend time on things that don't make any sense? It could be that we are still skiing along tracks laid by Taylor. Management make the strategies and 'rolls them out' for staff to execute. Job descriptions are clearly delimited, like the pieces of a jigsaw puzzle. We are cogs in the organisational machine. Taylor's ideas concerning the efficiency of production processes are easy to find in today's management and organisational *isms*.

In principle, technology can free people from tedious, mechanical and routine tasks to fulfil themselves using their natural capacities in creativity and empathy. As Esko Kilpi brilliantly said in his book *Perspectives on New Work*, published by the Finnish Innovation Fund (Sitra), the work of the future will consist of "interaction between interdependent people." The ability to interact is the key to productivity, and not just within organisations but in the networks that generate added value.

Such uses of technology is not a given. It is possible to imagine a future in which we harness algorithms to replace managers. In fact, that future is our present. Technology has made it easy to link remuneration to the fulfilment of targets, to the extent that a salesperson could be paid only for the times when they manage to make a sale to a consumer. Algorithms can be used to further tighten efficiency in ways Taylor could not even have dreamed of.

Which track will we ski down? Is the ox still our role model or can we re-establish the connection between thinking and action?

The sharp divide between theoretical knowledge and practical action, deeply rooted in our worldview, has led us astray. In the past hundred years, the work environment has changed dramatically, and few workplaces today remain stable enough to allow for detailed advance planning. Theoretical strategies and plans can no longer be separated from the practical contexts in which they unfold — nor can theory alone determine the shape of action.

I saw this dynamic firsthand during my time as State Secretary at the Prime Minister's Office in Finland, when we counted no fewer than 315 government strategies simultaneously in operation. In such conditions, centralised strategies risk becoming caricatures of themselves, while rapidly changing circumstances routinely throw a spanner in the works – weakening the vital connection between thinking and doing. As the saying goes, *"well planned is half done"* – but in today's reality, that often means it is also half *undone*.

Hierarchy does not encourage creativity but standardisation. Manager/employee relations involve a status threat and threats have been proven to hinder creativity (Edmondson & Mogelof, 2006). In other words, we are not at our best in front of our bosses, which is a shame for both parties.

The illusion of divisibility (and therefore categorisation) is a descendant of the two preceding illusions. We imagine things as being a product of the sum of their parts, just like one builds a car. As the vehicle body moves along the production line, it is equipped with the bonnet, the wheels, the engine. If the customer has ordered tinted rear windows, they are applied. If the windscreen is shattered by an errant stone, it is replaced. Living organisms and communities do not work like that. They are self-generating. There is no external designer or assembler who builds them out of parts; the parts interact and thus create continuous change.

Subdivision has been and will continue to be an important way for humans to strive to understand reality. Differentiation, division, specialisation, categorisation, delegation, allotment of duties, definition, standardisation and organisation: all these have facilitated evolution, civilisation, scientific discoveries and innovations. Subdivision becomes a problem when it becomes an end in itself and overshadows an element that is at least equally important: integration, i.e. making the subdivided items whole again.

We dismantle everything we can. You eat an elephant one piece at a time, they say, and you divide a strategy into sub-projects and development schemes. When we encounter a problem, the most common approach is to come up with a new budgetary allocation, role, profession or institution to take care of it. Once we have a separate profession or whole sector to take care of every problem related to being human, we will have completely subdivided humans themselves. We have our physical, psychological, mental, spiritual, social and historical dimensions, and each of these has numerous subdivisions, with the necessary people in charge.

Our vision of an organisation is, still too frequently, the image of a machine: it consists of successive layers of boxes, connected by lines, with fewer boxes the further 'up' you go. Fuelled by energy and capital, the organisation generates products or services. Production happens by recruiting workers to do specific jobs that create elements of the product or service. Once the parts are joined together, the product or service is ready to be delivered to the customer. The organisation grows through duplication. Workplaces are divided into specific areas, such as marketing, HR, finance, production and IT. We believe that scaling these same structures into larger entities will increase efficiency.

For the entity to come out in the desired way, efficiently, each employee's actions must be described, coordinated and controlled in measurable ways. Job descriptions, responsibilities, reporting, planning and budgeting all serve this end. The relationships between the stacked boxes creates the hierarchy of power and responsibility. The director's task is to run the organisation, make the strategy and execute it in a cascading fashion, by trickling targets down from one box to the next and compiling the resulting pieces of work. In this vision, the employee is like a mechanical robot connected to a factory's conveyor belt, stripped of human abilities or needs.

In today's workplace, jobs with carefully detailed job descriptions run the increasing risk of being made redundant by artificial intelligence, exactly because they were created more as parts of a machine than as ways of making the most of people's human strengths. Whether we see a work organisation as a machine or as an open system, based on the quality of human interactions, greatly influences the level of well-being, meaningfulness and motivation experienced by the people in the organisation.

The former leads us to seeing a lot of jigsaw pieces that do not form an overall picture. Social decision-making suffers from this, when the left hand does not know what the right is doing, and the various actions do not work towards the same aims. Workplaces suffer from this, when different units' targets and actions only lead to partial optimisation. The best way for one department to meet its targets is to shift its costs to other departments. Problems become evident at the very latest when customer service helplines become jammed with callers. In many public services, different experts take care of their own sectors without the citizens' needs ever being taken into account as a whole. If the parts are never integrated, the system will never learn.

The illusion of division has a strong impact on our views of the world and of humanity. Do we see reality as separate issues, things, people and events, or as a flowing process where individual parts are less important than how they are connected to the big picture, of which we ourselves form a part? When speaking of human communities, it is decisively important whether we focus on individuals or on their interactions. Is success earned separately by individuals? Are marginalisation, poverty and desperation the sufferer's own fault? Do we get what we deserve?

Of course, people should be celebrated and respected for successfully building their own life paths. No one can achieve success alone, however. The people around us, our community and the opportunities for growth and prosperity offered by society play a huge role in generating success. Where we are born greatly affects what we will become. Successful people have a lot to be thankful for.

No one should be blamed for ending up in deprivation or distress. We are not born with equal opportunities; different cards are dealt to us at birth, both biologically and culturally. There are systemic factors in society that can derail people into permanent difficulties. The idea of pulling oneself up by one's bootstraps demonstrates a total lack of empathy and context literacy.

Genuinely creating equal opportunities for all requires more than just offering the same things to everyone. Our starting points and needs are completely different, at both the individual and global levels. Understanding this and acting accordingly generates trust and fellowship. We are none of us architects of our own fortunes, so let us be facilitators of each other's fortunes instead.

The specialisation of knowledge and work has led to a lot of valuable advances in human and social development. As human cells divide and become specialised, they are able to respond to increasingly demanding functions, and the same logic applies to human systems. Cell specialisation is only one part of the process, however, because they must always be connected to a broader whole. The value of a single brain cell only becomes apparent when it interacts and is synchronised with other cells.

Cells not only work together but also repair one another, forming a more valuable whole than the sum of its parts. A person is not simply the combination of liver, eyes, brains and so on. Human development, including of the cognitive kind, is a process of differentiation and integration. The two elements contribute to our ability to adapt to an increasingly complex reality.

Humans have evolved the capacities of both the hunter and the explorer. We are able to focus on details while also retaining the ability to discern the big picture and new horizons. In today's world, we emphasise the focus on separate details.

In an ideal situation we would only subdivide to access things that are otherwise unavailable; we would subdivide to learn and to know, and then return the parts into the whole in order to understand and to act.

Growth is possible when specialised parts link back together. This does not mean stripping the specialist areas of their characteristics and mashing them together into a homogeneous blob. Integration maintains their specialist capabilities and connects them to achieve a better end result.

When the system encounters a challenge requiring a higher level of integration, but the conditions for integration do not exist, the result is the system's descent into either chaos or rigidity. The same applies to the human mind. When we come up against a challenge that requires connections between various parts of the mind but we have no ability to make that happen, we might end up either manic or frozen. This happens all the time and is seen not only on the individual level but also the communal and social levels.

After a long period of specialisation of knowledge and actions, more and more voices and initiatives are appearing that criticise our way of subdividing our problems and the knowledge required to solve them into ever smaller segments as an ill-conceived way of approaching the challenges of this millennium. Researchers in ecology, futures studies, integration theory, cognitive science, philosophy, psychology and complexity, for example, have identified how problematic it is to have fragmentation without integration.

The Illusion of Competition

WE UNDERSTAND *the economy* to refer to human interaction and to institutions related to the production, distribution, trading and consumption of commodities. *Capitalism* is an economic system in which the instruments of production – capital and land – are privately owned. The basic idea of the *market economy* is that businesses and households will solve any problems in the economy according to the laws of supply and demand, with free movement of capital and labour.

The market economy can be seen as Churchill saw democracy: as the best of all the bad options. It is efficient at allocating and reallocating resources to ensure a match between supply and demand because the market economy has an inbuilt self-correcting mechanism. For the market economy to work, it requires rules and regulations, for instance to safeguard competition and to prevent monopolies. Consumer legislation must ensure the symmetry of supply and demand.

Legislation has difficulties keeping up with the challenges brought by the development of the market economy, particularly globalisation. Individual countries are no longer able to regulate the actions of large companies as before, especially when it comes to the mammoth corporations that have sprung up in new, rapidly developing sectors. Global companies can pit countries against each other to see which one has the most tempting labour and investment conditions. This allows them to influence the development of favourable regulatory climates and production costs for themselves. As "winner takes all" situations become more common, consumers are left without options and monopolies arise where regulation cannot reach them.

The self-correction of the market economy has also proven insufficient when it comes to protecting the Earth's limits for growth. The logic of competition and economic growth acts as an incentive that does not sufficiently account for the limited nature of global resources or for the impact on long-term planetary well-being.

We love to think that the efficiency-enhancing impact of competition is a winning situation for everyone, but that is not a characteristic of for-profit competition. Usually the losers are overshadowed so that we cannot see them; sometimes to the extent that we are unaware of their existence. Many want to keep the child labour and inhumane working conditions of low-cost manufacturing countries hidden; the same is true of the impact on the environment. The for-profit game becomes an isolated board and nothing outside of it has any significance. The players feel that they must follow the rules and aim to win; changing the rules along the way would be unsporting.

Each player assumes a role according to which they play, and they stick to it even if it would be wiser or more ethical not to. "I just work here," or "I must think of the company and the shareholders, even if it feels wrong." It is a similar setting to politics, where doing the right thing and winning elections are rarely compatible.

Now we have come up against the planet's limits, however. The system's outcomes are unsustainable. We have a growing understanding that we can no longer toss costs and impacts aside for nature to deal with, without having to pay for them ourselves in the form of poorer living conditions. Emissions trading is a good example of how issues that are valuable for society are integrated into the rules and logic of the market economy. The competitiveness between countries makes it difficult to make global decisions on a national level. The inability of political mechanisms to prevent free riding slows down the advent of desperately needed overarching solutions. Self-correction does not work when the question is about revising the basic rules of the economic system.

When competition becomes the main framework for all activity, the idea of generating value is tossed aside by our desire to obtain as high a price as possible. Owing to its success, we have wanted to extend the logic of the market economy to areas of life to which it is ill suited. Then we come up against situations where the price that has been put on something does not match its value. We often erroneously see price and value as synonyms. Language, for example, is not anyone's property; it is owned jointly by us all and has great value, but no price.

Not all games end in a winner being declared. In his book *Finite and Infinite Games*, James P. Carse explains that there are games that are intended to go on indefinitely: that is the goal, rather than one player winning over others. Instead of gameplay according to roles, what is at stake is the changing self. Openness is a prerequisite and it is manifested in the vulnerability of the players, which allows them to live and learn in a changing environment. Surprise is a sign that the game continues, as well as an opportunity for growth. Are we trying to gain value from something for ourselves, or are we generating added value that will be generally available and will also benefit us? The difference in nuance may sound small but its impact on reality is huge.

Politics and economics are the forums of our shared decision-making and action. Both are permeated by the ethos of competition and winning, and visions of enemies. All of our worldviews are greatly affected by what our shared decision-making and economic systems look like: these forums have a significant impact on what happens in the school playground, for example, indirectly and subconsciously.

The constant competition for more money and more power is a major determining factor in how our world goes round. Although politicians and financiers understand the imperative of collaborating in our interdependent reality, neither game's meta-rules encourage it. Whenever the going gets tough, the cards related to competing and winning trump all others. As they infuse every activity, they become an end in themselves, justifying the means for as long as we dare to continue. Many authoritarian leaders around the world are pushing the limit of that daring further and further.

Being human is about far more than just economics or competing. Competition is based on a view of humans as separate yet identical units. These units are pitted against each other, and may the best man win. It is a vision based on opposites, objectification and isolation.

Working is also about much more than money or competition, even if the organisation operates in a competitive market. These days, market-driven competition has permeated workplace culture, becoming one of its defining features. It undermines employee well-being, erodes their sense of meaning, and lessens the real value of their efforts. If you want to get people to do a good job, give them a good job to do.

This illusion is also exacerbated by advertising, which sells us a belief in our value increasing in line with our possessions. At the same time, advertising trivialises love and friendship into elements of ownership and trade, a kind of zero-sum game. By eating or drinking our product, you will surround yourself with beautiful, smiling people. To succeed, buy this car. If you want to look sporty, use this shampoo. We tell ourselves that by acquiring things, we will become a certain kind of person. Advertising reinforces this illusion.

Amassing material possessions may fill physical square footage but not any inner void. You can't buy love, nor can you pay for meaningfulness in instalments. I have been privileged to meet many people who have turned their attitudes around, from receiving to giving. They speak with emotion and passion about all the important things that there are to share, whether it be through music, woollen socks, charity or life lessons for grandchildren. They are filled not with a void but with so much to give that they are in a hurry to empty their pockets and share their capital with others. Giving to others has granted them insight into life's purpose. Through giving, they are expressing their desire to grow as human beings within the time that they have left.

In this life, we often take the most important things for granted. Humanity is born of love, and formed within it. A parent's loving gaze turns a baby into a person – it is through being truly seen, with care and recognition, that we come to know ourselves as human.

But today, that foundational gaze of love – the one that affirms our worth without condition – has been displaced. In its place, we chase attention and visibility, hoping to prove we exist by being noticed. We mistake being watched for being seen. It's as if we've become a kind of pre-human creature, endlessly thirsty for the starter pistol of attention, yet never actually beginning the race.

Human spiritual growth is an example of aspects of life ill-suited to the logic of efficiency and competitiveness. The concept of human capital is a reflection of how economic thinking has been harnessed to describing and defining the process of spiritual growth. When it is parallelled with financial capital, we can easily get the sense that human capital, too, can be generated, transferred and directed according to production needs. We forget that human growth is a human quality, a slow and personal process that scarcely conforms to the logic of the market.

Many places around the world have long viewed schooling and education through the lens of industrial production: you put a child in school and after several years they will pop off the conveyor belt, fully formed and equipped with exactly the kinds of skills that the recruitment ads in the Sunday papers are looking for.

Something that is tightened to near breaking point will, in fact, break under pressure from change. Maximum efficiency brings vulnerability. Especially when it is combined with a hierarchical, siloed organisation, a process whose efficiency is maximised is brittle. Emphasising efficiency leads to centralisation, to markets ending up in the hands of very few corporations – as examples from online retail and social media have proven. At the same time, we become exposed to catastrophic risk. The shadow of efficiency can end up strangling us from behind.

The market economy generates the things it was created for. It is foolish to believe that it could lead to a different outcome if we just tweaked it a little. Economic competition and its incentives are like a game we are all playing. Even if we choose a different tactic, the game board, rules and winning strategy remain the same. Therefore it is necessary to scrutinise the game itself if we want the outcomes to be different.

The Illusion of Technocracy

I HAVE attended thousands of meetings discussing how to get people to think or act in specific ways. The assumption has been that those present at the meeting possess the correct and best opinions. Two types of solutions are usually proposed: either seeking authority figures (the Parliament, a university, celebrities, the media) to act and set an example on the basis of their status, or relying on enlightenment through reason (distributing information, holding talks, organising media campaigns, publishing pamphlets). Despite the committees' best intentions and commitment, these methods seem to have little effect.

Traditionally, authority and reason have been the most effective tools in the changemaking toolkit. The exercise of political or other types of power has relied on the idea that those with less power obey plans, orders and regulations passed down by those with more power. Status and the authority it bestows are crucial. Achieving change through power has a long history and was, in many cultures, originally legitimised by the idea of the divine mandate. Inheriting status from previous generations was also enough of a justification. Since then, subjects have been given a say in who gets to hold power, in the form of democracy and elections, and the limits of power are defined by law.

Bringing about change through authority is supported by sanctions that follow from a failure to comply with demands. Power is often justified in the form of knowledge: leaders are presumed to know more than followers, and authority figures are supposed to hold the keys to the common good, while subjects narrowly seek to protect their own interests. Leadership based on such power eats away at trust in authority. The more leaders are forced to rely on sanctions to make changes, the more they erode their trust capital. In systems based on elections, it means that the likelihood of change in leadership grows.

Emphasising power in trying to enforce extrinsic changes is less likely to spark an internal motivation to change. When the threat of sanctions is removed, behaviour may return to what it was before. The withdrawal of US troops from Afghanistan by the end of August 2021 sparked interesting considerations around the world: is it possible to change a whole nation's operating culture and value base by exercising military power? That twenty-year experiment, at least, said no.

Solutions that are implemented without involving the affected people are seen as hypocritical and thereby lacking. They fit everyday needs poorly. The authority figure does not, in fact, always possess better knowledge; the asymmetry of information often goes in the other direction. Decisions cannot automatically be turned into the desired changes, either.

Effecting change through reasoning is an ethos from the Age of Enlightenment. The starting point is a belief in the rational nature of humans: make evident the correct justifications and logic behind decisions, and rational people will act accordingly. Again, hierarchy is significant: some possess the correct information and reasonable arguments, and can explain them to make others see sense. Changemaking by reason works if people's mental models are already aligned with the proposed changes. If that is not the case, however, the proposed justifications are seen as contrary to beliefs and therefore incorrect. Those who already think the same way will act as desired; others will not. We humans do not act as rationally as we would like to think. We are good at rationalising our behaviour but not until forced to do so, either by our inner voices or by external pressure.

Seldom will a well-justified and desirable change go unimplemented for a lack of information. We have plenty of information, and yet we do not act on its basis. Our behaviour is led by other factors, such as our surroundings, the community with which we identify and our present circumstances. We may act in complete contravention to our best knowledge, because we fear losing something of value. People will no longer appreciate me, I will lose face, I will seem weak, I will no longer belong... We will stubbornly hold on to former behaviours, even when told that they are detrimental. We will not believe otherwise unless we ourselves find the old information to be incongruous with our reality and the new information to be a better fit.

So there are three broad options for someone trying to bring about change: to force and subjugate others to change; to force themselves to engage in intellectual sparring using arguments and reasoning; or to involve everyone in the changes from the start. This third model is based on internal growth and learning, and attempts to eliminate the power hierarchy. Changing by learning emphasises not only reason but a broader understanding, including the sociocultural norms, values, emotions and attitudes involved in the matter at hand. Motivation to change lies at the core.

Change happens when people change. The result is that people become committed to the solutions and integrate them into their identity. Spontaneous experience, reflecting on the experience and internalising what is learned can bring about a change in our mental models. Learning in itself is renewal and change. I will write more about this in Part Four.

More and more, the problems in our society are adaptive. That means their solutions cannot come from the outside; they require change from the people and other parties involved. There is no objectively correct solution, because the problem is tied to people's subjective lived experiences. Technocracy, or exercising power and reason from the outside, also misses the opportunity to utilise the mental resources and understanding of the nature of the problem and its solutions that is possessed by the people and parties involved in the problem.

In spite of all this, the power and reasoning models prevail when it comes to social – and even global – challenges. What does the illusion of power and reason tell us about those who use these models to bring about change? It is based on the decision-maker's vision of themselves as a machine-builder, an external maker of rules who lays down their authority and reasoning upon those who must change.

The ways in which we implement changes may have a bigger impact than the content of the changes themselves – it is a strategic choice. Changing by learning makes decision-makers a part of the system and influences how the system works in interaction with others. It helps us shed the illusion of technocracy.

The Illusion of Graduation

IN A book on the history of Finnish peasantry (*Suomen rahvaan historia*), Perttu Immonen writes about a late-seventeenth-century desire to build stronger foundations for the literacy and education of peasants: "Perhaps the most important breakthrough in terms of learning outcomes was to start teaching children instead of adults. Church documents demonstrate that children were more pliable before the growing demands of the Church. Each new generation developed into better readers and Christians than their predecessors." Ever since those times, efforts to teach and learn new things have focused on younger age groups. The idea that you can't teach an old dog new tricks has lived on tenaciously. You grow up by eating your veggies, going to school and putting up with the turmoil of adolescence. After that, you are done. Our belief in our mental and spiritual growth stopping hand in hand with our physical growth is still evident in the ways we build our education systems.

Research tells us otherwise. The plasticity of our brains remains through our lives, even if it slowly wanes with age. We can exercise our minds to keep them alert and flexible. Developmental psychology has also proven that significant changes can take place in our minds in later decades. This potential has remained largely untapped. Even though science has published its results, the ancient beliefs live on.

The time period required for innovations to spread and become rooted in everyday use has shortened significantly over the course of history. Print media achieved the milestone of 50 million users in four hundred years; television in thirteen years, Facebook in three years, and now OpenAI's ChatGPT in two months (Hu, 2023)!

It is not just about technology, either, but about the diverse pressures that our surroundings place on our thoughts, minds and selves. Networked humanity has become efficient at spreading its inventions swiftly to the whole planet – for good and for bad.

Previously, back in our school days, we could rely on previous generations passing on all the information and skills that the young would need at work and in their lives. In today's diversity of changes, this is no longer possible. Besides passing on our achievements in civilisation, we must equip coming generations with the skills to adapt to, encounter and solve challenges that we have no way of predicting. This is why general knowledge, creativity, curiosity, social and emotional skills, critical thinking and metacognition are increasingly important.

Even that is not enough though. We cannot rely on younger generations alone responding to our new circumstances. The ability and potential of adults to learn and grow mentally becomes very necessary. As external complexity increases, so must our own cognitive and moral complexity. In the village of my childhood, one could cope by learning the prevailing values of the community. Now that our horizons have broadened and contain diverse values and attitudes, moral and knowledge bases and a complex, continuously developing cultural and social reality, it is no longer enough. We must form relationships with these and be able to grow and develop our identities alongside the changing reality. Then the ability to think about our thinking, be aware of our shadows, understand diverse points of view and make ourselves understood is critical.

The challenge is huge, and diverse reactions are understandable. Some will withdraw back into the values of the village community, idolising them above other values. Others will denounce this and claim to rise above nostalgia by embracing a diversity of values in the name of tolerance. Yet others will declaim the relativity of everything, where nothing is more valuable nor real than anything else. Eventually both value and truth are denied and that becomes the only, superior truth. This is the shadow side of postmodernity. Supporting a certain set of values does not automatically make you right and all others wrong. It is possible to support something and still understand the value of other alternatives.

It is often said that young people must be taught new skills in order to solve challenges like climate change. It is true, but it is insufficient for many reasons. It is a slow road to change at a time when swift action is needed. It is also morally problematic to place problems caused by previous generations on the shoulders of new ones. Especially given that, with our own actions, we are consistently reducing the number of alternatives available to future generations. Acting in this way only increases intergenerational tension.

Ultimately, the example set by preceding generations also greatly influences the kind of culture that later generations build. If the model that they receive is of selfish behaviour that cares little for nature, why would they be motivated to act differently?

For these reasons we must consciously make use of the abilities for spiritual growth of adults. I am not talking about work skills but of a broad process of human growth, which gives us opportunities to blossom as employees, family members, community members and global citizens. The labour market and the society at large need rules, models and infrastructure that provide funding for supporting adults' inner growth.

In her book *The Nordic Secret: A European Story of Beauty and Freedom*, philosopher Lene Rachel Andersen describes the rise of the Nordic countries from agrarian communities into industrialised democratic welfare states, from the 1860s onwards. She believes that the popular education and folk schooling institutions that arose at that time, focusing on people's inner and spiritual growth, played a major role in allowing the Nordics to make such a significant social development leap peacefully. What could we, in today's circumstances, learn from those experiences from 160 years ago?

When the pressures of spiritual well-being and humanity grow beneath the complexity of society and reality, our need for being equipped with tools for mental, moral and emotional growth and identity development is tremendous. It can also be justified in terms of labour market needs, because many professions are also encountering growing needs for broad-based abilities instead of today's narrow expertise. This is demonstrated for instance by a 2021 survey conducted by McKinsey of 18,000 people in 15 countries, concerning the foundational skills that will help citizens thrive in the future of work (Dondi et al., 2021). Adaptability and coping with uncertainty were the proficiencies that were most strongly associated with employment prospects.

It is time to raise the "Nordic secret" from beneath its invisibility cloak and up to the pedestal it deserves. We should consider what new opportunities and forms we could have for supporting growth among adults. It will allow us to find solutions for global challenges. We have left this huge spiritual potential untapped for far too long.

The Illusion of Anthropocentrism

LANGUAGE IS revealing. The word *environment*, when used to describe nature, places it outside of and around us. It emphasises the speaker or subject as a separate being from the object. This is how we are used to looking at the world. Nature is viewed as separate from us, created to serve us. We have turned ourselves into divinities, masters of all we survey. We value ourselves more highly, as superior and wiser beings than all the other beings in creation. We have entitled ourselves to exploit nature as we see fit. We believe we can control its evolution and ecosystems like we control a lawnmower. It is only in the last fifty years that we have awakened to the fact that this worldview is based on a treacherous illusion.

The idea of man as the master of the world springs from the individualistic worldview where each individual sees themselves atomistically – as separate and special. This has also led to a strong tendency amongst some dominant groups to separate and subjugate different groups of people, as well. Race, gender, religion, ethnicity, sexual orientation and other forms of diversity have been used as justifications to bestialise people, to turn them into inferior animals who are not entitled to the same rights as other humans. Although a lot has been done, and many achievements have been made in human rights, the attitude is still rife today. We come up against this ideology on a daily basis.

We have become disconnected from each other, both near and far. Our kinship with bygone generations has also weakened, along with our understanding of their influence on who we are today. Nor does the continuum with future generations awaken enough of a sense of responsibility for the consequences of our actions.

Similarly, we have become disconnected from nature. Various symbiotic and parasitic relationships can be found in ecosystems. In former times, humans lived in a kind of symbiosis with nature, understanding and respecting its vulnerability and its ability to recover. It might not have been an ethical choice, but a question of the imperative of safeguarding nourishment and shelter and fear of the forces of nature. We should be wary of over-idealising former human generations' relationships with nature, because awareness of the planet's limited natural resources has only been available to us in modern times. Previously, there was always an opportunity to move to new territories, and find new resources.

Through industrialisation, humans took a controlling role in this relationship. We gradually developed into a parasite that is killing its host – in this case, our very ecosystem. Humans and our cattle make up 96 per cent of the mass of all mammals on Earth. Wild animals only account for four per cent, and 70 per cent of all birds on the planet are farmed poultry (Bar-On et al., 2018).

According to ecologists, extinctions due to human activity have multiplied a hundredfold since the year 1900, and we are currently in the midst of the Earth's sixth extinction wave (IPBES, 2019). Because the extinction of any species is irreversible, the metaphor of taking on a divine role is justified. We cannot predict the knock-on effects that the extinction of a single species will have on the bigger picture of the world. It is impossible to know what chains of events will be sparked off by the disappearance of one organism, influencing – possibly fatally – the organisms that interact with it. We humans are not beyond these chains of events, either.

In a *Special Report on Global Warming*, the Intergovernmental Panel on Climate Change (IPCC, 2018) cited more than 6000 scientific publications to demonstrate that the time is up: this is our last chance to act. It was the highest-quality data, collected, analysed and laid before our eyes. Limiting global warming to 1.5 degrees Celsius would signify a much better life for people on Earth than a rise by two or more degrees: fewer diseases, better crops, fewer floods and natural disasters, maintenance of biodiversity, smaller masses of climate refugees and less of a shortage of clean water. Although the difference of half a degree higher may sound small, its impact is in no way linear: it would bring about a massive leap to an agglomeration of interdependent negative consequences, causing a significantly worse situation – for us humans.

Could we try to do our best as communities, nations and global citizens to safeguard living conditions on Earth without being forced to do so by a large-scale disaster, duress or suffering? Each of us according to our abilities and opportunities, with our best intentions? It is a question of how much we appreciate and value the future – even that which will come after our passing. Are we prepared to grow to ensure that the reality we leave behind is better for future generations and the environment than what is indicated by our current path?

Right now, we are in the lobby, the waiting room, and we don't know what lies behind the opening door. It is high time to ask ourselves: are we the parasite that destroys the ecosystem in which it lives, causing its own demise, or a species capable of living symbiotically with the rest of nature, making use of it but without causing irreparable damage?

The Illusion of Knowing

"Why does hair grow on our head?" "Why don't animals have to wash their hands?" "Do bacteria have germs?" Finland's biggest newspaper publishes children's science questions, and together with the obituaries they make up the most genuine content in the papers. The experts who respond are as childishly enthusiastic about answering the questions as the children are in asking them. They summarise scientific truths comprehensibly, inspiringly and without embellishments. Knowledge is a tricky thing. Some things we know through evolution, without being taught – for example, being wary of snakes. Other things we know through teaching. Learning always implies adapting to the outside world. We learn that when the pavements are icy, we should walk with care or wear spiked shoes; or be even more creative and apply salt or install heated pavements. Then there are things we claim to know, even though we don't actually: we "know" our neighbour's telephone number, but only because it is saved on our phone. We outsource our knowledge. We might know about blockchain technology because a relative works in a company that uses it. We know "through each other".

We live in a fairy-tale world of knowledge. What we call knowing is often believing or trusting. Search engines and the growth in computerised memory capacity make us think of ourselves as all-knowing. Our knowledge is only put to the test in practice – through doing and experience. Lengthy power outages caused by winter snow in Finland, for instance, have demonstrated the demise of many everyday skills that people used to possess to survive without electricity.

Do you know how a flushing toilet works? It's simple, you say, but take a piece of paper and write down or draw the workings of a toilet: what goes in which direction, and powered by what? Knowing "in principle" is not enough.

We spend all day thinking. We spend less time considering or obtaining an understanding of *how* we think. It is just one of those automatic functions. We brush our teeth twice a day, but how often do we brush our thoughts? Almost all our successes and failures, as individuals and a species, depend on them. Ask anyone about their thinking skills and they are likely to answer, "It's just something I do."

Many self-help books exhort us to "listen to your inner voice, trust your instincts, always believe your thoughts and emotions." I don't recommend it. Our thoughts and emotions are often incorrect. We should doubt them and expose them to critique – just as we do others' opinions. Why should my thoughts and emotions be fully formed from the start, when others' are not? It feels good to be right, even when we know we are wrong. And if we are proven to be wrong, we expend huge amounts of energy developing arguments to demonstrate that although we were wrong, we were actually, under certain conditions, perfectly right.

Does what you know and think make up your identity? Everything we know, we know conditionally, "until proven otherwise." And the proof is constant, right down to the simplest things. Many "flat earths" can be found in our thoughts. Hence we should not base our identities on our thoughts, or we may end up persecuting those who believe the Earth is round as infidels. Attaching our selfhood to knowledge is dangerous, because then we throw down our anchors and forgo any future, possibly superior, ways of thinking. Instead, prepare for a journey of the mind, with ever-evolving scientific knowledge as your staff.

American courtroom dramas torture the viewers' sense of justice when the defence lawyers clutch at any straw that protects the defendant, ignoring clear evidence of their guilt. It is pointless to become indignant about it, because we all do the same. We think about the things we believe. We gather data and arguments that support our opinions and ignore evidence to the contrary. We are the defence lawyers of our opinions and there is no fact-seeking judge present. Therefore, we all need each other to correct biases in our thoughts. We seldom manage to stick to helping, however, as a different motive will soon appear: it feels good, while proving someone wrong, that you can simultaneously prove yourself to be right. Double the joy!

Our minds are more than our brains. Neuroscientists tell us that by exercising our minds, we can alter our brains. We can change our thinking by practising different thoughts. It's worth taking common sense into our hands, to turn it over, look at it from different sides and note its strengths and weaknesses.

The author G. K. Chesterton once quipped: "I've searched all the parks in all the cities and found no statues of committees." Even in knowledge, we idolise the individual. And yet, in many academic disciplines, the number of co-authors of papers has doubled in just a couple of decades (Henriksen, 2016). Many articles in the science journal *Nature* have more than one hundred authors. The same applies to this book: probably none of the thoughts herein are fully my own. I have found them in dialogues, books, articles and lectures. What is my own is my way of combining various thoughts and opinions and putting them into words. No one on this planet has read the same books while having had the same childhood in Eurajoki, western Finland, having spent time as an exchange student in El Paso, and being in possession of the same genetic heritage.

Each of us has an individual path that makes us unique. When unique people get together to know things, valuable ideas are born. Knowledge is not a personal resource but something that is organised within an environment, in certain tools and in interpersonal relationships. How well we cope with the future depends on what use we can make of each other's competence and shared knowledge. It has been our saviour through evolution; humans can be "us" just as naturally as we can be "me".

So how can you learn to know better? Firstly, familiarise yourself with the thing you want to know about. Then, acquaint yourself with kids' science questions. Physics Nobel Prize winner Richard Feynman has a studying technique named after him, which includes writing the information down as if you were explaining it to an eight-year-old. That will keep you from deceiving yourself in using jargon that even you don't understand. Putting things simply requires in-depth knowledge. When you notice gaps in your learning, you will have identified the limits of your knowledge. That will allow you to seek ways to move those limits further. Finally, test the technique on a real eight-year-old!

For many decades now, we have claimed to live in an information society. Information is a critical production factor. Decision-making is based on information, and a lot of money is invested in generating new data and subsequent innovations. Truth has become an ideal, and the processes that threaten it are now often known as the "post-information age".

The scientific worldview and information based on academic research methods have been a success story. The teachings of the Enlightenment have achieved a foothold all around the world with many benefits. The nations that are content with maintaining peaceful international relations fight battles on the field of competitiveness, and their weapons are innovation and know-how based on new information. However, while science and academia have been crucial in permitting problem-solving and the development of communities and civilisation, the emphasis on the scientific worldview has not been solely positive. In focusing on rational knowledge, it has overshadowed (often violently) other kinds of knowledge and ways of knowing that humanity possesses.

We might define knowledge in relation to our observations and perceptions through the senses and our processing of this empirical data. But, more precisely, this is known as *propositional knowledge*. Knowledge is a justifiable, true fact. For example, a dog is a mammal because it gives birth to live pups which it feeds through mammary glands. A group of animals that share certain characteristics that distinguish them from other animals are classified as dogs, and numerous observations have allowed us to conclude that birthing live pups and feeding them with milk are also characteristics of dogs.

This kind of knowledge comprises facts about reality generated by scientific methods. Science has developed tools, theories, techniques and aids that support our limited sensory perception. The person doing the perceiving and the object of the perception are both parts of the interaction that generates knowledge. Propositional knowledge fuses into our semantic memory.

Professor John Vervaeke of the University of Toronto has identified a further three types of knowledge:

Procedural knowledge is knowing-how, knowledge of how to do something, which arises by practising and perfecting certain skills like riding a bike. It is not a question of perceiving truth but of an agent having mastery over their interaction with their surroundings. *Perspectival knowledge* is knowing-from, based on the emotional, mental and bodily state in which one finds oneself and allows us to imagine what it would be like to be someone else and/or in a different situation. *Participatory knowledge* is knowing-through, in which we are one with our living environment and exist consciously in our surrounding reality, sharing the flow of life.

Vervaeke describes our time as one of a crisis in meaning. He believes that meaning cannot be found in propositional knowledge, but only through the three other types of knowing. The essential thing is to have an embodied presence in reality and the ability to act in interaction with our surroundings. The feeling of meaninglessness of life arises from a loss of connection with any type of knowing other than the propositional.

Over human history, in moulding our worldviews, we have gradually cut our ties with the holy by claiming that because its existence cannot be proven, it must not exist. We have cut ties with our own agency and conscious decisions with the theory that there is no such thing as human free will, and that the brain's neurobiological machinery makes all decisions before we take any action. We have cut out the idea of our actions having an effect on life after death through certain religious claims that salvation is a matter of mercy alone, not human action. We have isolated ourselves from the rest of nature by putting ourselves above it. We experience separation and estrangement and suffer from addictions and anxiety because our connection with ourselves as psychophysical entities is deficient.

Vervaeke's epistemology grasps something essential and deep about the flipside of the overemphasis on scientific and academic knowledge. Conceptual knowledge is valued over experiential knowledge. We have come to believe that the map is the same as the territory; that abstract concepts and scientific data are equal to reality. In our yearning for control, we want maps of everything, a complete cartography. Our need for efficiency and dominion have motivated us to manipulate the map, and now the erroneous map markings are starting to show in the form of spiritual unease, anxiety, bad decisions, the meaning crisis and estrangement from ourselves and from society.

As pure information or scientific data without understanding of the nature and dynamics of interaction are incomplete and may lead to flawed conclusions, we need a shared language and method for describing interactions in a complex system. Systems researcher Nora Bateson came up with the concept of *warm data*, which she defines as "information that is alive" (Bateson, 2021); a knowing of the interrelationships that integrate elements of a complex system. It is a qualitative counterpart for *cold data*, which is quantitative and measurable. The idea of warm data becomes critical when decontextualised scientific data is returned into its context, where it encounters the perspectives of other scientific disciplines, as well as experiential and other forms of knowledge.

The emphasis on knowing is so ingrained in our societies that it leads to many other kinds of misunderstandings. In focusing on the importance of knowing, we express confidence in the conclusiveness of knowledge. As we conquer more epistemological territory by laying down foundations of knowledge, do we actually reduce the terrain of ignorance? No. We simultaneously reinforce both our knowledge and our insight into what we might not know. Our understanding that there are myriad *unknown unknowns* grows. The role of science is to shed light on uncertainties and reveal the areas we know nothing about, where ignorance reigns. First, we must become aware of our ignorance in order to form a reasonable belief about the truth.

It is not knowledge but ignorance – and the ensuing curiosity – that is at the core of finding new information. The biggest questions in life are mysteries: death, love, the human journey, consciousness. We do not know whether knowledge about them even exists. They are essential to humanity, however, and our minds seek answers to and relationships with them. Scientific knowledge cannot provide these. It can research and process them as phenomena, but we need different methods for understanding and accepting them.

The Nigerian–Finnish author Minna Salami considers the theme in her book *Sensuous Knowledge: A Black Feminist Approach for Everyone*. She believes that we worship reason. Since modernity, we have been conditioned to believe that all truly valuable knowledge is rational and logical. It is not seen as something that can be accessed and evaluated through the arts or the related emotions and sensory and bodily experiences, for example. The arts are associated with talent but not knowledge, Salami claims. "Yet art is also suited to explaining reality because art captures reality from the inside out," she writes. "Art explains who we are because our existence is artful. We are not simply rational and mental beings, we are also emotional and physical beings. Art is a way to understand and change reality just as much as quantifiable information is." Salami says that "civilisation thirsts for humanistic thinking as the Sahara is thirsty for water." She uses the term 'Europatriarchal knowledge' to describe the prevailing dominating and mechanical vision of knowledge, which devalues anything erotic, feminine and poetic because they spring from the elemental, natural world. Wisdom is found in more rounded 'kaleidoscopic' thinking, in recognising values traditionally dismissed as feminine, as well as in the African worldviews that Salami parallels with Greek mythology (Salami, 2020).

I do not know if the term "post-information age" is justified. Did we ever live in an information age? Were decisions formerly based solely on information, and was regard for information central to societies? Perhaps we have become more aware of the numerous biases and weaknesses of our thinking and information processing, which we never cared about before. Maybe the weakened role of our traditional knowledge bases forces us to become more conscious of what our views are based on – if anything.

When information starts to be used as a weapon, the significance of information becomes emphasised in what information we accept and reject. We become predictable as individuals, identity groups and interactions between groups. We are like robots that know one language and fail to react to any other. Unfortunately, this is not a situation that can be solved by providing more information or by practising scientific literacy. Research has shown that improved scientific literacy does not reduce the influence of one's own identity group in forming our opinions (Drummond & Fischhoff, 2017). This is why increasing knowledge and skills is not enough; we need to motivate people to strengthen their inner incentives. We need the motivation to critically consider our own thinking, to recognise our thought biases and to consciously alter our ways of looking at the world. Striving for truth can equip us to cut loose from the cycle of self-delusion and self-deception. Consciously seeking out the company of people and groups who think differently is an excellent way of practising this.

I believe that many people share the feeling that the scientific worldview does not answer all the questions that we would like it to. Instead of defending and closing in on itself, science must take steps forward; engage in creating new understanding. Science and the philosophy of science must learn to renew themselves amid the present challenges and defiance. The worst that could happen would be to have all energy and attention going to safeguarding the current status of science and research, when what we need is for the role of science to be clarified and complemented in relation to our complex reality and the broader question of what it means to be fully human.

The Illusion of Relativism

IN *THE Republic*, Plato divided society into three classes: labourers (farmers, craftsmen, builders), warriors and philosophers. Leaders should be chosen from the last group. People are on the same level in principle, but few are capable of attaining the virtue of reason. Plato's classification corresponded to a tripartite division of the human psyche: where labourers tended towards passive desire (*appetitive soul*), warriors displayed enthusiasm and discipline (*spirited soul*) and philosophers demonstrated rational wisdom (*rational soul*). In a Platonic republic, justice was done when each class of people took care of its own duties and stuck to its roles.

This division into classes has been adapted through history, and the classes have been renamed, but the basic idea has stayed the same. Some attempted to justify slavery based on such a division. The interplay between groups has followed the ideas of leadership by power and reason, and the role of the lowest castes has become obedience. Some have claimed that the division into classes is God's will or fate inherited at birth. Eugenics was the extreme manifestation of this manner of thinking. The class division that happened as part of industrialisation and its counter-movements – the class conflict – brought the issue to the heart of social policy. In many countries, we still speak of the upper, middle and lower classes in our everyday language.

In other words, humans have throughout history felt a need to organise society and people hierarchically. We are now undergoing a stage of reorganisation. Hierarchies are out of fashion. They appear to us as ladders, where those who stand higher up are stepping on the fingers of those below. No wonder the ladders have been toppled over where possible. Openness and transparency have shed light on the fusty corners of power, and the idea of doing things according to established customs has been consigned to history. *#Metoo* is a good example of how an oppressive culture can be highlighted and start to be demolished with the help of publicity.

Many oppressive hierarchies remain, and new ones are created as old ones topple. The new ones can be dangerous in their subtlety: social media with its tribes and bubbles, for example, is a veritable ladder factory. Having a group identity is valuable, as long as it is not seen as superior to other groups' identities in the sense of "we are chosen ones, better, more correct, more faithful than they." Opposition, painting enemy pictures and rising above others make group identities very problematic.

Are all hierarchies dangerous? The concepts of goodness, truth and beauty involve hierarchies; civilisation forms a hierarchy; laws are inherited hierarchies. The question is, are they oppressive or freeing; exclusive or inclusive? Hierarchies based on subjugation deserve to crumble, but what about ones built on inclusion and growth? When all hierarchies have been undermined, it has led to research data becoming relativised. The context-specificity of truth has slipped into truth being tailored to suit every person's needs. There is my truth and your truth, and that's that. That's equality for you.

The aim of demolishing hierarchies springs from the idea of ensuring freedom. This way of thinking feeds a self-centred worldview and an endless, vacillating discussion with no way out. The fact that every point of view contains something of value does not mean that all points of view are equally worthy. If nothing is more valuable than anything else, even scientific data cannot rise above other things. Without our ladder, we cannot reach the roof from where we can see further and wider.

With belief in the certainty brought by the Enlightenment waning, our time has sought alternative ways of being in touch with reality. Intuition has become popular. We trust our gut feeling because it is a part of us and therefore boosts our lacking self-confidence. Intuition is like a concentrated form of experience, and while it is valuable in problem-solving and everyday life, it can mislead us. Our strengths can also be our weaknesses. Unless we are practised in thinking about our thinking and recognising its biases, intuition can lead us by the nose. Intuition often results in stereotypes and preconceptions.

The shared contract of our social institutions – legislation – has been granted the power to use public authority to promote the things that the society views as valuable. Although we do not often see it that way, our maternity clinics, schools, health centres and universities, for example, are expressions of power that also limit civic freedoms. The objective of this limitation is to permit growth and the fulfilment of freedoms even better than before. These institutions represent the hierarchy of growth. The cultures of many growth-oriented institutions have over the centuries included – and unfortunately still do include – hostile elements. Springing from good intentions does not guarantee that something cannot be used for evil. The basic idea was to invite participation, to raise up everyone, to enhance inclusion. If we demolish our institutions of growth we will quickly descend towards everything being relative, to ultra-individuality, to a world that twists into narcissism via cynicism.

The great Finnish philosopher Georg Henrik von Wright (1971) spoke about the worldview of acceptable pluralism, a multi-perspectival approach to knowing. He did not mean that everything should be relative with no universal scientific truths, however. A lot of continuing social dialogue is still needed for us to form a shared vision of what acceptable pluralism might mean in various times and places.

The Illusion of Permanence

THE GREAT challenge of our time can be illustrated in the form of a packet of chocolate cookies on the table in front of us. Eating the cookies brings pleasure here and now, whereas the prize for leaving them untouched may be associated with weight loss somewhere down the line. The fact that they are there, within reach, challenges our willpower to such an extent that short-term pleasure often prevails. The same logic guides our actions when it comes to climate change and many other behaviour-dependent challenges. The choice between allocating resources to basic or applied research is another example of the same phenomenon. A belief in being able to harvest the fruits of applied research more quickly erodes the soil beneath the basic research that is needed for growing them.

The Covid-19 pandemic drew attention to the concept of resilience. The ability of humans, organisations and nations to cope and survive, possibly even stronger than before, was set as a desirable target. Many said that we must not let a good crisis go to waste. The pandemic proved that maximum efficiency-seeking in companies' value chains had weakened their resilience and made them vulnerable. A sparseness of resources meant that some public services were unable to bear the changes caused to the operating environment by the disease. We lacked the necessary resources for preparing legislation because they had been minimised to a level that allowed us to just about cope under normal circumstances.

Efficiency and resilience are not contradictory, however; they are the same. Only the time scale separates them. Resilience is efficiency in the long run, whereas the efficiency that we seek – which has now proven itself vulnerable – is in the short term.

Many roll their eyes at the insanity of people taking payday loans. Of course, it sounds crazy to make decisions that will only worsen the situation further down the line. It's unbelievable! Or is it? In their book *Scarcity*, Harvard Professor Sendhil Mullainathan and Princeton Professor Eldar Shafir demonstrate how people do not always behave rationally. Especially when something is scarce, our ability to make sensible long-term decisions suffers. The authors show how poverty, for example, can reduce one's mental performance as much as a sleepless night can – and anyone who has suffered from insomnia knows that the next day is hardly ideal for making important decisions. With too many worries, our minds cannot operate sensibly. Our slow, long-term deliberation does not work if our main goal is just to survive until tomorrow. The research in the book contributes a whole new perspective on poverty and marginalisation. When you suffer from a lack of money and work, the scarcity itself decreases your ability to make a living, even in the future. This is why permitting poverty and marginalisation to go on is a travesty – not just in terms of human suffering and inequality, but also of the wasting of our shared capabilities.

The same problem of reduced performance can be extrapolated to the national level. It was known from the 1990s onwards that in the 2010s, Finland's working-age population would experience an exceptional reduction in numbers. And yet, as a nation, we were incapable of making the necessary decisions to prepare us for the situation that is now at hand. The national deficit cannot continue growing at the current rate, but it never seems to be the right time to decide on adaptation strategies. You cannot do it in a recession, because you only increase people's difficulties and hamper economic growth; in times of prosperity, however, things are going so well that there is no political pressure to do it.

In social services and healthcare it would be sensible to shift the focus from fixing problems after they arise to taking preventive action. Similarly, it would be wiser to react to climate change sooner rather than later. Still, we delay making decisions – and not just on a national level, but globally.

Our major issues are ones that cannot be solved in a single electoral term. It will be a question of decades of effort. With regard to climate change, the years 2035 and 2050 have started to appear frequently as target years for decision-making. Climate scientists look at developments with an even longer lens. One electoral term is barely enough to get started. But the longer we delay decisions, the bigger the problems become.

The situation is a challenge for our political decision-making system. Democracy may be the most workable of our known political systems, but it has its failings, too. Elections lead to decision-making being divided into electoral periods. The world does not operate in four-year cycles, however. Longer initiatives and projects do not fare well when they fail to fit the four-year attention span. We need a greater temporal diversity of solutions: quick short-term trials that give us information and knowledge on best practices for the future, as well as road maps for longer-term joint commitment.

Elections mean that there is little time for making and preparing decisions. After elections, it takes time for lawmakers to organise themselves and learn to bear their responsibilities. Time is wasted running aground a couple of times before the new people learn that instead of rushing, it is worth preparing things carefully. By that time, the next looming election is starting to lower the motivation to make decisions. Decisions will only be made when it is imperative, in a hurry and in a way that will keep us in office after the next election. In fact, these actions are just like those of people taking payday loans. In the European Union, decision-making is always difficult because one major member state or another is about to hold an election, so big decisions cannot be made.

Elections are the self-correcting element of democracy, but at the same time they are the field on which the competition for obtaining or holding on to power is held, which sets the real rules for decision-making. The incentive of gaining votes is strong. The private sector is often criticised for its "quarterly capitalism" and profit-orientation, but the same applies to politics: what party would forgo an election win on the basis that it is achieved by means that might undermine the democratic system in the long term? Corporations have started talking about their social responsibility and, although it might sound silly, political parties should do the same.

Long-term decision-making increases complexity. Clear and simple solutions do not fit well within long-term goal setting, which requires extensive shared commitment to progressing in a determined direction. Even single parties are demonstrably bad at committing to long-term policies. They lack the incentive to do so, because they don't know whether they will be in government or the opposition when the time comes to implement them. They do not want to limit their future room for movement, which is logical in itself, but it prevents the nation from agreeing on a shared long-term direction.

Researcher Teppo Turkki (2015) has studied the development of East Asian countries over a long period. He has observed strategically functional decision-making systems that are based on intelligent execution and factual data, and found that they share one feature: they are not democratic. It is a challenge for us defenders of democracy. How can we ensure that the system that gives every citizen the power and freedom to be influential produces results that will continue to justify its own future existence?

A good example for democratic systems was set by the National Assembly for Wales in 2015, when it passed legislation obliging it to ensure the well-being of future generations. The Future Generations Act means that Welsh public bodies must make decisions in cognisance of their long-term effects, work in greater partnership with people, communities and each other, and do things in pursuit of removing tough problems such as poverty, health inequality and climate change. The system's own meta-level rules were changed in a way that generates a process and responsibility for longer-term reviews and value choices.

Overtraining is a state where excessive exercise leads the body to stop developing physically, and any further training starts working against itself. The body's performance weakens and the athlete is taken over by physical and mental fatigue. Overtraining is often caused by a dependence on continuous training without sufficient recovery time. Although people understand the importance of rest days on a factual level, the feeling of inferiority arising from missing an opportunity to exercise can stop them from making reasoned decisions. For a fitness addict, overtraining may be impossible to avoid, even if they are aware of it. Their mind draws them to the running trail time after time, because they believe their value as a human depends on continuous training.

Similarly, there are other areas where we become immune to the changes that our senses tell us to be necessary. In their book *Immunity to Change*, developmental psychologists Robert Kegan and Lisa Laskow Lahey describe how certain changes, although we are aware of their necessity, become impossible because change involves fear and an assumption of losing something dear to us. We stay in the hamster wheel of economic competition because we fear we will no longer be valued otherwise. We want more for ourselves because we do not want to be worse off than others. We strive to control life because we fear what will happen if we let go. Even though we know delegating decision-making responsibility is wise, we stick to making detailed decisions so that our colleagues will continue to admire our capability.

Imprisoned by the worldview built by the ten illusions I have outlined, we are overtraining ourselves. By overemphasising one point of view, we become blind to the bigger picture. This reduces our performance and our ability to live safely through change. It is like training a couple of muscles and letting the rest atrophy while believing we are on top form.

It would make sense for us to exercise the muscles we need to fight the challenges that lie ahead for humanity. Right now we are exercising the ones that are mostly causing the challenges.

We may have escaped from being at the mercy of nature, but we have set the Earth on a trajectory towards destruction. Humanity has initiated biodiversity loss and climate breakdown whose ramifications are unknown to us. Competition has generated short-term efficiency but made us vulnerable to crises by reducing our resilience. By subdividing and specialising work tasks we have solved numerous problems, but we have forgotten to integrate them in order for the system to work as a whole. We have conquered unknown terrain but lack understanding of the openness and emerging nature of complex systems. We have made incredible accomplishments in science and civilisation, but have warped our attitude into *egoism* instead of *eco*-ism.

The human ambition and success in escaping the clutches of nature were major steps forward in our ability to control our own lives, and gave us freedom to take the next steps. Attaining these goals, however, has made evident the price we have to pay for our freedom. Shifting from being under nature's control to controlling nature ourselves has impoverished nature's diversity. Sticking to our former goal stops us from seeing our own shadows – from integrating the various aspects of thought and knowledge and expanding our idea of our relationship with nature towards a more sustainable form of interaction.

We have ended up holding the illusions of rationality and human superiority, a mechanical vision of nature, the world and civilisation. We have projected all of the wonder of the external world onto ourselves, but it is now time to redirect our sense of wonder to the broader spectrum of life. Our illusions have contributed to generating risk agglomerations and we must apply ourselves in every way to stop the full disastrous effects of the metacrisis.

We have to make use of our as yet underused abilities. Our worldview must be broadened so that we can better understand ourselves and our relationship with nature. We must create new tools and processes of collective wisdom so that the larger goal – preserving life on Earth in all its interdependence – can be fulfilled.

There is no centre of balance in the middle of a dualistic worldview. Any attempt to find one is doomed to fail.

The system freezes and the path permanently enslaves us.

Sometimes it is worth taking off our glasses to check how dirty they are.

It would make sense for us to exercise the muscles we need to fight the challenges that lie ahead for humanity.

What makes snowfall so fascinating is the number of crystals, their size and density, and the way they dance with the air as they come down.

Reading the news, we subconsciously ponder who is the villain and who is the hero of the piece.

We are still waiting for the clear and nasal tone of the oboe.

Part Three: Potential

Q: What is the world asking us to become?

A: Wise. But we need our idea of wisdom to evolve with our new planetary context, and to manifest in new institutional arrangements.

1. *We Are in the Unseen*
2. *We Are with the Unknown*
3. *We Are Our Shared Uniqueness*
4. *We Are the Ever-Present Ending*
5. *We Are the Others We Don't Know*
6. *We Are Our Rituals and Routines*
7. *We Are Ongoing Creation*
8. *We Are Our Sensitivities*
9. *We Are Our Expanding Perspectives*
10. *We Are Systems Learning*
11. *We Are Uniformity and Diversity*
12. *We Are Democracies Learning to Renew Democracy*
13. *We Are Reimagining Governance for a Planetary Context*
14. *We Are the One and the Many*

We Are in the Unseen

LED BY illusions, we have ended up where a wise person would never have found themselves. We must now live up to the name of our species, *Homo sapiens*: the wise human. We can achieve that by utilising our social nature for goodness, beauty and truth.

The situational picture I have drawn in the preceding chapters raises two main challenges for humanity in our time: 1) shifting from an individual-centric vision of humans to one that values the interaction between individuals; and 2) integrating the global identity that the planet's limits have made inescapable, into our self-image.

Humanity may be reaching for the stars, but from very shaky foundations. The ten illusions share the idea that what we can see, control and measure is all that is valued and all that exists. Furthermore, the financial and political power linked to managing it keeps this idea alive. The rebuilding of our current nation-states and Western societies after the Second World War was a victory march for that ethos. Now humanity faces the question of whether we have taken this successful and fruitful strategy too far. Are we so path-dependent that we cannot tell when the environment has become unfavourable for our strategy? The researcher Clayton Christensen calls this phenomenon *competence-induced failure*.

At a species-wide level, we must become sensitive to understanding the status quo, including the changes in our environment, form a shared willingness to step off the trodden path and reallocate our mental and material resources. The duty of politicians is to prevent violence, wars and conflict escalations – not to fuel them. The aim of human interaction must be to foster the good and the potential in each other, not to cause them to shrivel through competition and subjugation.

Ikebana is the Japanese art of flower-arranging. Its principle is to bring together humanity and nature through the careful arrangement of flowers and other elements. It developed from the sacrificial floral arrangements created by Buddhist monks in temples. Japanese friends have encouraged me to look at ikebana as works of art, and doing that has taught me a lot of valuable things about life. The thought of pausing before a flower arrangement to consciously focus on what I could see seemed at first like a waste of time, infused, as my ego was, with the Western ideals of efficiency and rationality. Gradually, however, as I spent time looking at an arrangement, I found myself being altered by it.

We could learn a lot from the art of ikebana. Looking at a flower arrangement, we can reflect on each plant or their combination and try to understand what else it can tell us beyond being a pretty bouquet. Ikebana experts see the arrangement as a process that starts at the bottom, with the stems, and tells the story of life with its various stages and branches. Besides the plants themselves, one of the crucial elements is the empty space consciously left between them. That tell-tale space ties together the visible branches or leaves. You cannot understand the story of the whole without understanding what is left out.

In our material, atomistic and control-obsessed worldview, we have learnt to focus on the concretely visible. What we don't perceive does not exist. A lot of fundamental things are then left beyond our understanding. We emphasise the physical over the spiritual. An organisation's recorded strategies and plans are highlighted at the expense of the operating culture and organisational taboos. Explicit knowledge triumphs over tacit knowledge. Emotions, values and attitudes, social norms and factors that are fundamental to the nature of interaction, such as trust, are trampled by written norms. We fail to read the message of the empty space.

Music tells a similar story and can be a more familiar point of contact for many. Music isn't about individual notes. Our experience of music arises from the interrelationships between the notes; how they are played together and what kinds of empty spaces and pauses their narrative includes. What lies between the notes is more important than the notes themselves. When the instrument is a whole symphony orchestra, our experience arises from how the arc of the music builds up, with its numerous themes, into an entity where the separate elements are only significant as parts of the whole. All this is fulfilled by the players and the conductor, interpreting the composer's vision in mutual interaction, perceiving both the movements and the pauses of the conductor's baton and reacting to each other's expressions. While it requires perfectly honed professional skills from each individual, the crucial components are not the individuals but rather what they do together.

The same applies to all human interactions. We know that bringing together the world's top experts will not necessarily generate the world's best results. Besides expertise, what they need is an ability to work together, to understand each other and their diverse perspectives, to learn together, to consolidate their various points of view and to catalyse something completely new. All those things are more important than the individuals' personal expertise. In Finland, we are well aware that the teams that have brought home the Ice Hockey World Championship cup have not actually been dream teams consisting of the best individual players in the tournament. Instead, they have earned the title thanks to skilled coaching, good team spirit, joint commitment, competent role allocation and excellent interplay.

As discussed in Part Two, in complex environments, reality is an open, continuously changing, unpredictable, interactive and nonlinear, infinite game that has us entangled within it. Becoming connected to each ongoing situation so that we learn from it can help us to heal some of the lacking connections from our interactions. It is no coincidence that we now speak a lot about service design, user orientation, joint development, experimentation and ecosystemic approaches: the vocabulary springs from a novel understanding about how we can learn through interaction and what design will be like in the future. Our ability to adjust to the situation is crucial: we must understand the significance of the interrelationships between the parts of the system, as well as the properties of the system itself.

We have to be able to harness our inner potential – as both individuals and communities – as a resource for our outer journey. So far, that resource has been woefully underused. Our current attempts at moving forward are like those of a boat without a sail. Our capacity for human growth could be the sail that lets us navigate towards a more sustainable future.

We Are with the Unknown

IN THE summer holidays of my childhood, as soon as I opened my eyes in the morning, my first thoughts were of worms and fishing rods. Breakfast was only a delay on my way to fishing. My parents had to come up with a tactic for ensuring that I would eat before going out: they thought of using some old bowls from our summer house, with colourful pictures on the bottom. Whenever you took a spoonful, more of the picture would show and you could try to guess which one would be revealed today.

Research by the esteemed neuroscientist Lisa Feldman Barrett (2020) has suggested that our brains work with that same logic. Brains continuously guess at what will be revealed and what will occur next; they utilise recollections of what has previously happened in similar situations, and on that basis they transmit energy or neurotransmitters in anticipation of what will soon be needed. The external reality perceived by our senses and bodily messages is supplemented by guesses of what overall picture is about to be revealed. Emotions are also a way of preparing for a coming event.

When situations are repeated, our brains get used to reacting accordingly. Gradually, I learned to know the pictures on the bottom of the bowls and could guess from the tiniest hint what would be revealed. We learn to have certain emotions in certain situations, and that model stays with us. If we feel discomfort performing before an audience as children, the feeling follows us into adulthood. Our brains' reactions and guesses concerning the energy needed by the body in anticipation of what is coming will become established unless we make a conscious effort to feel a different way. We can affect our own feelings more than we believe, and in fact we are the only ones who can do so. Reconnecting with our self-knowledge can be a way to heal some of the separations created by the illusions of our worldview.

Insecurity and uncertainty are not synonyms. Certainty can only be achieved in perfectly unchanging situations, and we do not want those. It is a useful mental exercise to consider what it would actually mean. If on my summer holiday mornings I had known exactly what picture would be revealed in my porridge bowl, how many fish I would catch and what else would happen during the day, I would have been unlikely to bound out of bed. There would have been no tingle of expectation or excitement, no surprises, no hopes, plans or dreams.

We must not take ourselves too seriously, or that will be the only thing we have time for in life. We hold beliefs that reduce our well-being and our ability to reach goals, and yet we hold on to them for dear life. Our parents, friends and living environments have helped by telling us what we were like as children or what we are like deep down, repeating it to the point where it becomes self-fulfilling. After that, our inner voices ensure that we never forget these characteristics. Goethe said that, "If you treat an individual as he is, he will remain how he is. But if you treat him as if he were what he ought to be and could be, he will become what he ought to be and could be." The same applies to how we treat ourselves.

We Are Our Shared Uniqueness

ONCE, WHEN I was out for a walk, a man came by me with a boy of about five who reminded me vividly of how I imagine myself to have been over half a century ago. I was taken aback. What if he had been me? What would I have wanted to say and to hear? Would it have been the same person I feel I am now?

Today's world tells us: "Be yourself. Be authentic. Have the courage to be your true self." The true inner self has become inestimably precious, and yet finding it is harder than ever. According to researcher Rasmus Mannerström, identity crises affect people of all ages (*Helsingin Sanomat*, 30 September 2020). Suddenly, adolescence reaches from acne all the way to varicose veins. Parents are able to foresee the beginning of adolescence and be prepared to act as lightning conductors, to give their beloved child room to grow into themselves. But what about when flying into a rage and having emotional meltdowns becomes the norm at any age? Who will be our lightning conductor then? What will happen to adulthood?

Life's comprehensibility, meaning and manageability will be tested. In a continuous crossfire of alienating world news, external expectations that lead to a constant feeling of inadequacy, a lack of time to take care even of life's basic tasks and an inner voice that questions whether any of this makes sense, our self-image can feel buffeted as if by a pressure washer. In a world where image is critical, being authentic is complicated. It is not enough to be authentic, because you can be inauthentically authentic, and only authentically authentic is good enough – unless you are authentically inauthentic, which is acceptable, unlike the pathetic inauthentic inauthenticity…

Discovering our identity is the crusade of our time – and like the actual Crusades, it is used to justify injustice. Terrorists are recruited with promises of dignity, salvation, access to ideological purity or entry into a religious community. They are all building blocks of identity and therefore dangerous. Black-and-white explanations of the world are attractive, especially if they offer a protective new community to someone who has been marginalised, bullied or dismissed.

We often link our identities to our thoughts, believing our thoughts to be our own. We believe that thoughts (which are beyond our control) are ours and parts of our identity. When we wake up after a good night's sleep and something that worried us yesterday has been resolved overnight, as if by magic, who has resolved it? If our consciousness and identity are equal to our thoughts, who can take credit for solving something in their sleep?

It is hard for us to reconcile our concept of the unchanging identity with the ever-changing reality around us. Identity is not what we are by ourselves but what we are in interaction with each other. It is kinder to ourselves to consider identity as something adaptable that is built in relation to the surrounding community and its people, growing along the way.

Learning to know ourselves is not a one-off exam we have to pass but a continuous journey of understanding. The genes we receive and the culture in which we are born interact and mould us. The possible combinations of nature and nurture are infinite, and that hones our uniqueness at each time. However, our uniqueness encompasses a blind spot. When we look at the world, we see the landscape before us but not the eye looking at the landscape. It is not just about our senses but also our mental models. We perceive the things that are recognisable by our minds; we see the things we expect to see. Focusing our attention is a moral action that creates both light and shadow.

We love to present the good in ourselves and to hide the bad. As it has become more common for people to live alone or in small families, it has meant that we are surrounded by fewer and fewer people who really know us. In contrast, there are more and more people further away, who only see the good parts of us that we want to show. This hides our capacity for evil even from ourselves. This other part of us follows us like a shadow, however, and if we do not accept it, it becomes a blind spot – a part of us that has not been integrated. We don't know ourselves. We often project the characteristics of our darker sides onto other people and see them as weaker, less valuable or contemptible, when really what we fear is the unknown, hidden power in ourselves.

The style of dialogue that is currently gaining strength, in which we destructively use our power to see faults in each other, turns our gaze away from our own shadows. When our weaknesses are fed, our ability to separate our own points of view from others' also weakens. We become egocentric. Our spiritual growth is stymied by a wall built by the ego. By recognising how, in certain circumstances, each of us is capable of evil, we can take a step towards shortening that shadow. It allows us to shed light on a larger part of our selfhood and to form our own ideas and opinions, regardless of the influence of our social groups.

It is easy to convince ourselves of our empathy by empathising with people we agree with anyway, because they belong to the same group. In reality, we are then prisoners of the group mentality – egotistical together and easy targets for identity politics. Our empathy is actually put to the test and needed when we encounter diversity.

Knowing ourselves implies an ability to see oneself with an outsider's eyes. We must step into another's shoes to reflect on ourselves, and in doing so we reinforce our skills in thinking about our thoughts, feelings and behaviour amid and in interaction with everyone else. The ability to reflect on ourselves, our thinking and our experiences is a critical way to develop personal wisdom: we learn not only about our similarities to everyone else but about every person's uniqueness. We learn to process our reactions to various situations, to encounter surprising circumstances and to regulate our behaviour and emotions.

Self-knowledge is seen by many as the recipe for successful living, but defining success is like putting a ladder up against the wall of life. Success tells us which way to climb if we want to be valued. We search for things where we can excel over others – be prettier, stronger, richer, smarter, more famous, higher-flying, more sociable.

There are fewer handbooks on how to cope when success wanes. What happens when our presumed superiority takes a downward turn? When wrinkles take our beauty, muscles begin to atrophy, sickness eats at our strength, younger people steal the attention and retirement eliminates our professional cachet? Our economic possessions may remain but as we get older we also gain understanding of our inability to take them with us when we go. So it is all downhill from here. Our achievements will be as forgotten as yesterday's paper. Will that make us less? Has our time passed? What will happen to our selfhood if it is built on a narrow definition of success? Will the memory of success make us thirst for ways of boosting our self-esteem again and again until we become old and embittered?

In the next fifteen years, the only age group that will be growing in volume in Finland is 74 plus (Tilastokeskus, n.d.). Some theorise that the evolutionary reason for the lengthening in our life expectancies is that we will need the experience and wisdom gained from ageing to solve the challenges that jeopardise the survival of our species. That idea speaks against diminishing as we retire.

Research has found that people who were seen as gifted in their youth rate their mental well-being lower than others at the age of 80 (Casino-García et al., 2019). While many former top athletes, artists, scientists and celebrities understandably grapple with this, the phenomenon actually affects us all. If your identity is based around success, you could be looking forward to some unhappy times.

Unhappiness makes us prone to addiction, whether it be to constant hurrying, mind-numbing intoxicants or consumption. An addiction speaks of an inability to live with oneself. The opposite of addiction is connection: with oneself and with others. Connection is an experience of oneness. Therefore, it makes sense to build our identities more broadly than the narrow bases in which self-help guides would have us believe.

A meaningful life is not based on surpassing or outrunning everyone else, but on doing good. Superiority over others should be replaced by a more solid connection with oneself, life and other people. The gift of climate change to the development of human identity is that it directs us away from the material towards spiritual growth, and from egocentricity to interaction.

We Are the Ever-Present Ending

ONE PART of self-knowledge is being able to relate to the end of one's life. Few things in life are as certain as death. As surely as the sun rises, each of us will see the day when our breath becomes just air and the beating of our body wanes and stops.

Death is life's great mystery. It is the end point for our being, doing, belonging and knowing. It gives rise to fundamental questions: What am I? Where have I come from and where am I going? What is the purpose of life? Religions have tried to offer understanding and rituals for coping with these larger-than-life questions. Does death equal salvation, the start of a new life, a road to Heaven or Hell, the end of everything, the expectation of resurrection or a path to shared enlightenment? Our concept of death greatly influences our worldview. For our control-hungry culture, death is a bitter pill. Can one speak or write about it, or is it better to say nothing? Does it feel hard even to read about it here?

Death is associated with fear. What is it that we fear in it? I was not alive a century ago and I am not afraid of that time, so why should I fear the time a century from now, when I will not be alive? I believe it is a question of premature loss of life, or no longer having agency and losing something significant. The fear of death is the agony of surrender.

Death is often associated with weakness, giving up, loss, getting our dues. Seen in that way, it makes sense to sweep death under the rug, turning it into a lonely disappearing act to keep ourselves from having to face its likelihood. That lets us think about life as winning, invulnerability, individual immortality. Everyone knows this is a lie. Death happens continuously within us: things that no longer work, die off, and eventually the whole body will stop working and we will perish.

The knowledge of death generates a need to achieve something. The passage of time gains significance; when our time is limited, things become meaningful. Tales of people overcoming serious illness or near-fatal crises to awaken to life's true meaning are some of the most enduring stories. Realising that one's days are numbered is portrayed as the reason behind a change in lifestyle. Is it necessary to visit the gates of death to realise one should live?

If there were no death, the world would become overpopulated, or we would have to stop reproducing. The immortals would be the last children, youths, adults, elderly people ever to inhabit the world. Never again would the engendering of new life from love, the birth of a child, the marvel of growth, the joy of parenthood, be fulfilled. Awareness that each of us is equal in the face of death increases our understanding of equality. Death is indispensable for the things that we hold most meaningful and dear in life; death is a friend to being and to birth. It is sad, sometimes tragic, but it is the prerequisite to new life. When I die, I hope I will turn into fertile soil or ash, from which something new can be born.

It is the same way I try — and often fail — to live: striving to facilitate the birth of new opportunities. It seems meaningful to me to live such that the future I leave behind has a greater chance of prospering. It is a kind of sustainable growth.

We Are the Others We Don't Know

THE COVID-19 pandemic gave us a good lesson in how oppressive it is to be physically separated from other people and how meaningful socialising is. It made me ponder what kinds of companions we are to each other. The instrumentalisation of personal relationships is not unusual in our time.

Introducing ourselves to strangers, we are likely to tell them about our professions and backgrounds. Then each will form a stereotyped image of the other. This method is an efficient use of our attention and energy when we meet a lot of people, especially if encounters are brief. The flipside is that we imagine ourselves to be right in typifying people. Having spent years commuting by train, I have mentally classified people on a daily basis. Eventually, when I have summoned the courage to get to know my fellow passengers, I almost always find my preconceptions to be wrong.

These days, when we meet people we know, it is customary to emphasise our efficiency by remarking on how busy we are. Really stopping to listen to another person is rare. We need separate retreats or discussion groups so that we can be aided in listening to each other. We spend most of our days staring at diverse screens and judge the people we see on them from the outside, without having to submit to interactions in which we might reveal our vulnerability. We know various TV characters' lives better than our neighbours' names.

There are people among us whom no one ever looks in the eye. Their outward appearance makes us draw swift conclusions and turn our heads, because looking someone in the eye is an act of seeking and demonstrating trust. We do not treat them like people. Perhaps we fear that by looking in their eyes we will encourage them to speak or to ask for help, and we want nothing to do with them. Perhaps we fear what will be reflected in their eyes, or are ashamed of how we are likely to behave and do not want to see ourselves in that situation, so we would rather abscond. These invisible people in our daily lives are living proof of how much room there is for growth in us, as people and communities.

We yearn for wealth and fame, even though we know that they hardly ever increase anyone's happiness. An eighty-year running study by Harvard University has shown that the factor that most clearly correlates with happiness is good relationships (Solan, 2017). So why do we seek happiness everywhere else? How could we change our ways and discover healthier relationships with others?

We Are Our Rituals and Routines

A GAME is only fun when you take it seriously, however paradoxical that sounds. It can be hard for adults to immerse themselves in games – hands reaching out for smartphones and minds drifting off. This is why, often, adults prefer games such as escape rooms, where "survival" depends on conscious presence. Similarly, rituals are only meaningful if we take part consciously. Otherwise we become puppets led by the ritual – servants to the form who merely wonder when it will all end. A ritual should not be slavery to a habit but a transformation into something new. We can all try what it feels like, while keeping the door open to what went before, in case the change feels too substantial.

A morning cup of coffee is a ritual that has become routine for many. It wakes us from our torpor, helping us shift from night to day via a pleasurable custom. We humans are *normal*, i.e. fulfillers of habitual norms. Our daily routines and habits should represent the ways in which we would like to live and spend time. Instead of routines leading us into exhaustion, we should build ones that raise us up. Breaking poor routines is an act of everyday heroism. Transgenerational behaviour models – where one generation after the other acts in the same way – are even more demanding. If there were awards for such things, medals should definitely be handed to those who dismantle damaging transgenerational structures. That is real heroism.

When asked about the secret to a long marriage, many elderly couples will talk about routines. Always kiss your spouse in the morning, never go to bed angry, say "I love you" even when you don't feel like it. Is that inauthentic, dishonest? Perhaps sometimes, but they have valued sustaining a deep connection between them more highly. Routines that are put in practice generate microscopic changes in our desired direction of life. Rituals are also an opportunity for shaking up routines. They can briefly transform life, and us. We can connect and become part of something larger.

Human relationships are demanding and people are complicated. Maintaining good relationships is tough, but highly rewarding. Humans are deeply sociable beings. We need each other; we become human through each other. "Being yourself" doesn't work by yourself. Creating genuine connections with other people helps us understand ourselves and generates meaning for our lives.

We Are Ongoing Creation

I WOULD like to have been a fly on the wall, back when there were no flies or walls. More specifically, 13.8 billion years ago, when the universe began expanding in all directions from a single point. The beginning of everything. The Keeper of Tabloid Superlatives, if there had been such a person, would have been left scratching their head when none of their usual clickbaiting words – *huge, massive, mega, ultra, greatest-of-all-time* – would have sufficed to describe the scale of the Big Bang.

The world's richest people are currently competing to conquer space, looking for another planet that could sustain human life. Earth has perfect heat, light, gas, gravitational and climatic conditions for us. At an earlier age, my naïve assumption was that this was a fortuitous coincidence. Having appeared on this planet was like winning the lottery for the human race. But nothing is as wonderful as realising how wrong you have been; of course it is no coincidence. Humans have evolved over time in interaction with their environment, and it is we who have adapted to the environment's conditions.

If we had adapted to life on the largest of Saturn's 62 moons, Titan, we would move about on or inside dark organic sludge, rocks would be ice, rain would be liquid methane, and on a mild day, the thermometer would show −179 °C. We would have come out pretty differently in that environment!

But I am not alone in my incorrect assumptions; a similar worldview has actually been prevalent for a long time, even after Darwin's revolutionary theories came to light. The default premises of our cultural doctrines change slowly. We still act as if we were separate from our environment, immune to its alterations. We have stuck to our mechanical worldview, in which Man is the ruler of the machine, above and beyond everything else.

The environment into which infants were born a century ago was very different from today. Still, with their parents' help, they have the capacity to learn to latch onto the environment's clues as tightly as their fingers latch onto anything they can reach. Interacting with our environment and possessing solid learning mechanisms allow us to survive and adapt in accordance with our surroundings. Babies are born with the keys to survival.

Tomorrow morning, when you squeeze your stripy toothpaste onto your brush, consider how it got there. Over five thousand years of hygiene and health knowledge, product development from hog bristles all the way to today's nylon brushes, and a paste consisting of ten to fifteen ingredients brought from all over the world and extruded into a tube that your spouse says you squeeze from the wrong place. All that is human creation!

We see the Big Bang as a fairytale-like story beyond our comprehension or even our telescopes, that friendly TV physicists might tell us about. When did the Big Bang end? It never did; it is still ongoing. We are a part of it.

We live in an open system where chance, certainty and choice all overlap. We are always both creators and the created. Being human implies tension between us and our environment. We are human when we feel someone's touch; when we let our pulse relax amid the peace of a forest; when enthralled by the rhythm of music; when wondering at the beauty of summer; when enjoying the taste of coffee. Those are examples of the equalising nature of humanity: we share in our uniqueness.

When we miss the 'good old days', could our nostalgia for golden times actually be a yearning for a connection with ourselves and with nature? Can the good old days be found in our younger years or does that feeling spring from a subconscious longing for a prehistoric development stage? The myth of Adam and Eve relates that by eating from the forbidden tree of the knowledge of good and evil, they are banished from the Garden of Eden but gain knowledge and awareness of themselves. Suddenly, fig leaves became necessary.

We are in a hurry to know things and find solutions. We don't have the patience to stay in the revealing state of ignorance, which makes room for hidden emotions, intuitions and perspectives. It is less about acquiring information and more about opening our hearts, minds and wills to new things.

We Are Our Sensitivities

A RT CALLS us towards reality. It is a different kind of knowing. I am referring to poets, painters, dramatists, dancers, musicians and authors; professionals of sharpened senses. Should we listen to those who are sensitive enough to be among the first to recognise the unsuitability of our present reality? Some can see the dissonances created by our self-centred and competitive vision of humanity, our culture of materialistic relationships and our short-sighted exploitation of nature. Some have not yet formed a thick enough skin to be untouched by events in the external world. Some minds are under strain; and their job is to discern things in reality that science cannot reach, through art.

One of the essentials of being human is our relationship with ourselves, other people and our surrounding nature and culture. Interaction is everything. From our first breaths we are connected with our surroundings. Our identity and self-image develop through empathy with others. Connection, physical touch, being accepted as members of a community and a balanced relationship with nature are parts of our physical and mental safety net.

We must stop seeing sensitivity as a weakness and understand its strength. It might be what saves us. Sensitive people are often the quiet ones, and so their voices are not heard in this chaotic auction house of life. They might possess the most valuable message: that which tells us where we are going wrong. The ability to be heard and have their say can help to heal those who feel broken. Therefore, it is time to start listening.

Conflicts between people arise from looking at different things from different perspectives and at different distances, and yet believing that we speak of the same things. Each of us has an incomplete understanding of reality. We see reality through the lenses of our experience, personality, education and other competences. The same issue can be seen from one's own, another's, the community's or the whole system's viewpoints. Reflections can be made on a single level or we can try to integrate them all into the same reality. All levels and perspectives may simultaneously be true and yet cause conflicts and fights; even violence.

Our way of understanding reality has the same effect. Take, for example, the reading of a text: some will read words and sentences mechanically, without fathoming their content. Others will read them literally, as individual words and sentences that describe reality. Yet others will look at the broader story that they form and its arc, and some at the symbolism hidden between its lines. When we see reality in such different ways, it is hard to find a joint basis for understanding. None of the ways is more correct than the others, but their results are different. This, again, is Vervaeke's 'perspectival knowing': the ability to recognise what it might be like to be something or someone else.

It is a human's nature and role to grow and change. We change as our environment changes. How we approach that change critically affects how we view our agency, how happy we are and how well our personal frames correspond to our external reality. Becoming more sensitised to the changes happening within us, between us and around us is a vast potential that we are going to need.

We Are Our Expanding Perspectives

UNNECESSARY CONFLICTS could be avoided through the use of constructive dialogue. By listening and seeking to understand how others see the world – their assumptions, perspectives, and levels of observation – we can filter out the issues on which we don't truly disagree. This frees us to focus on the questions that are rooted in value choices, where diverse viewpoints must be considered in order to reach a shared strategic intent.

Ideally, we want to aim for equal rights and opportunities for all. That is far from the starting point, however. The hardest structures to topple are those that are so inbuilt into our language and worldview that they go unnoticed.

I learned this as a young man, as assistant to Finland's then Minister of Education, Riitta Uosukainen. Now that it was my duty to look at things from her perspective, I gradually started to discern small nuances, sayings, gestures and nonverbal communication exchanged fraternally between men that dismissed her as a female minister. It was astonishing to notice a reality of whose existence

I had not previously been convinced. It was equally startling to realise I belonged to a group that, so imperceptibly yet skilfully and effectively, wielded power over others. After that experience, I have never looked at the world in the same way. Naturally, Uosukainen claimed her place and wielded her own power, but she had to work harder for it than her male colleagues.

Even today, violent clashes and conflicts between groups around the world are derived from decades, even centuries, of hierarchical and oppressive structures passed through the generations. Power achieved through oppression is never sustainable. A price is paid for it, first by the oppressed and later by the oppressors. Both sides are prisoners of the oppressive system.

When the challenges of our time refuse to be solved by answers passed down from above, we need new models for moving forward. As I have said previously, we cannot know how someone else experiences things, but through interaction we can practise empathy and compassion and can develop our capacity for considering multiple perspectives.

Instead of atomistic egotism, which emphasises the differences between people, we must focus on what happens between people. It is important to learn how others think. It is said that shaking hands developed as a way of ensuring that the other person did not wield weapons or sweaty palms (which would indicate evil intentions); a firm handshake was a message of honourable trust. Today, we need similar, extensively applicable customs for ensuring each other's intentions. To some extent, the norms of urban environments fulfil this task, allowing us to spend time among masses of strangers while trusting that they will not hurt us. Far from increasing trust, social media appears to narrow it along with our cognitive flexibility, while also creating dependencies on attention and acceptance.

The pervasiveness of competition causes human relationships to become instrumentalised. Imagine you are driving to an important meeting and are already running seriously late. You try to make up for lost time on a busy road. Suddenly the other drivers become slowcoaches, Sunday drivers, road obstructions and total losers who can't even find their gas pedals or gear sticks. Now let's imagine you meet the same people in a library or at a child's school play. They turn out to be really pleasant people, fun and polite. Are the same people really that different in the two situations? It is not actually about them at all, but about you and me. We judge people based on whether we see them as obstructions or facilitators on our journey towards our goal.

Our individualistic worldview idolises each person's own objectives and expectations. When we value them more highly than other people, our fellow humans will be reduced to simple obstacles or tools on our journeys. The common good starts to sound like an old-fashioned conceit. That is the direction in which we are moving. We will lose out on the collectivity of the human experience. Each person's needs and desires are important, but so is the ability to reconcile diverse needs, while taking into account people's equal rights and opportunities. Our quality of life and achievements are the result of joint efforts.

We Are Systems Learning

THE NEED for joint effort is why it is so important to understand human systems. Seventy thousand years ago, humans were a species that did not particularly stand out amid thousands of others. Now, we are the only species that has managed to spread throughout the globe and take control over the planet's reality, for good and for bad. It has not been thanks to individual people's achievements: we can thank our ability to work together in target-oriented fashion. The crucial factors have been creating sophisticated cultures beyond the foundations of biology, and being able to pass on what we have learned to following generations.

We must understand how the complex systems formed by complex people work to be prepared to meet the challenges of our environment. An example can be found in the world of education: it takes a village to raise a child, as the African proverb goes. The child's parents play a crucial role, but so do teachers, schools and the other professionals involved. Friends and extracurricular activities also play a part. How can these different agents be connected together to serve the child's best interests and needs? Behind each individual lie a number of organisations with their own objectives, including the society's educational, social service and healthcare systems. If these agents cannot collaborate to serve the ever-changing needs of a growing child, the child will suffer – regardless of the best intentions of each separate instance.

Acting separately, the sum of all the different organisations will not be favourable. A favourable outcome requires the ability to connect with the child and their emerging growth environment, in a network of agents. The joint objective of supporting the child's growth creates an interdependence between them of which they must be aware.

Our human system is built out of interrelationships and may contain diverse subsystems. With regard to a child's upbringing we can speak of the systems of the child themselves, the family, various service providers, decision-makers, professional groups and guidance mechanisms. The levels involved are that of the individual, their close circle, the region, the nation, the continent and the world. Systemic change can happen in multiple dimensions and often does, simultaneously – physical, metaphysical, epistemic, social, political and psychological.

When legislation changes at the national level, it does not automatically lead to better outcomes popping out at the other end of the system. The child will continue to live in the same system. The outcome depends on whether the legislative change alters the whole system's interactions in a favourable direction for the child. This is often difficult to predict. Therefore, it makes sense to involve the other agents in the system in formulating a suitable solution. This ensures their commitment to it.

In other words, the system changes when the nature of its interactions changes. If there is a significant difference in views on a child's upbringing between school and the home, the interaction will be characterised by tension and a lack of agreement on what is best for the child. If the school is far removed from social service and healthcare professionals, they will be unable to share important information related to the child's best interests. If the authorities have an established, shared view of the "correct" course of action, there will be little room for the opinions of parents and other involved parties, and tensions may escalate. Whether the different agents in the system speak the same language or not is one of the crucial factors affecting the tension. Besides such physical facts, the nature of interactions in the system is also affected by different worlds of experience and the level and type of constraints in the system.

Consciously generating and dismantling tensions indicates the system's ability to learn. What is the system's field of interaction like? Whose voice needs to be heard more loudly? What tensions are there between and within the system's various levels? How can the distances, differences and similarities between the interactive relationships be modified in the desired direction? While we look at these questions together, the system changes and a new cycle of learning can begin.

In human systems, any certainty has a finite, usually short lifespan. Ashby's Law of Requisite Variety is a hermeneutical model, according to which the levels of variety within and outside a system must correspond to each other, otherwise the system will implode. Another way of putting it is that maintaining a system with limited room for movement takes a lot of energy which will, at some point, run out, causing the system to be destroyed. North Korea's attempts at keeping its citizens closed off from external influences indicates that tension is growing between the levels of internal and external variety in a way that will eventually unravel.

A total lack of tension is not the desired state in a system either. As in human physiology, the balance achieved by a complete cessation of movement actually means death. Learning and adaptation stop. When speaking of live humans, tension is a property of systems that allows for dynamic development. How to achieve balance between coping with tension and maintaining functional ability is one of the challenges of this continuous flow. The phenomenon is sometimes described as being "on the edge of chaos." (Packard, 1988)

Organisations should be made more human. Striving for good is an ethical choice that humans make and room should be left for that. As machines replace people in routine work, humans are left with tasks that require our core capabilities: ethical, situational thinking; problem-defining and solving abilities; creativity; interaction skills; and ways of determining meanings and purpose.

These qualities will become as significant as capital for the future of organisations. Employees are no longer in place to mechanically create parts out of shapeless entities; each person is there to fulfil the organisation's mission with their human contribution. Having a power hierarchy is not the primary purpose behind being organised: arranging the interaction that is essential for generating added value and success in the work is. Being organised is not making an annual reshuffle of boxes but a continuously emerging process of how to work.

In today's operating environment, the challenge is how to combine a vision of diversity and variety as assets with the creation of cohesiveness and a shared framework within which those assets can be fulfilled. Instead of carefully defining what each member of the organisation should do, it is more important to determine what no one should be doing. It is the same idea as that of old folk tales with their morals: they didn't tell you where to go but where not to go, leaving other alternatives open for the listener to decide on.

Performance management is the prevalent way of achieving the desired targets, especially on the public side, but the challenge with that is our rapidly changing operating environment. When the context changes, the things that seem most crucial for performance may lose their significance. Performance targets are set individually or for the organisation, even though their fulfilment is rarely dependent on the actions of a single expert or organisation.

In a rapidly changing environment, capability management is a more reasonable technique to use than performance management. It refers to governance and leadership that strives to reinforce a responsible agent's ability to connect to emerging challenges and to find optimal methods of adapting, together with others. Leadership focuses on boosting the resilience and learning culture of the organisation. It is a perspective shift from solving problems to developing the system; instead of believing that problems can be solved using the right solutions, we believe in work that aims for the development of the system, to optimise the fulfilment of its mission.

We Are Uniformity and Diversity

I CANNOT presume to reflect on the lived experiences of others. But the recent story of Finland, which I *have* lived, is illustrative of broader global patterns, challenges and opportunities.

At the end of the last millennium, Finland still had a largely uniform culture. Most people shared similar values, experiences and daily lives, and worked towards similar dreams. In the past couple of decades, the diversity of our values and lifestyles has increased. While we still presume to know how Finnish people think, we are increasingly often wrong. Finns are much more diverse than the stereotypes that are held about us. Our external appearance and our sociocultural backgrounds do not tell the truth.

This has been evident in public discourse for a long time. From "surely no one thinks that way", reactions have evolved towards, "that is the wrong way to think." It is too easy to say, "You're wrong; that is not how to think or vote" and then to believe we have fixed everything. It has been done before, and it does not result in the desired changes; it will only escalate differences. Populist movements, extremism and the post-truth era are all consequences of something. It is easier for us to ascribe consequences to causes than vice versa; we choose to focus on the consequence when we don't want to face the cause.

In Finland and elsewhere, there are large groups of people who feel like outsiders. Our faith in progress did not follow through for them; they found no refuge in it. They ended up invisible, with no one hearing, listening to or meeting them.

When there is a multiplicity of causal relationships, people will yearn for simple solutions. Political ideologies that fit in a nutshell (and should stay therein) feel safe for some. Voters should not be underestimated when it comes to complex issues. According to Einstein, "everything should be made as simple as possible, but not simpler." That is difficult, but fundamental.

The diversification of worldviews, values and attitudes places the operating models, status quo, target-setting and decision-making of the Finnish society before new challenges. We are not alone in that; similar challenges are felt around the world. Finland differs slightly in that we used to be uniform, and that trust used to play a significant role in the society's functions. If we fail to maintain a strong basis in trust in our new circumstances, Finland stands to lose even more than many other countries.

We Are Democracies Learning to Renew Democracy

DEMOCRACY IS a self-correcting and self-directing model for shared decision-making, but a demanding one. To work, a democracy requires an education system that guarantees citizens the competence they need to participate; a quality media environment that can generate reliable dialogue and situational pictures; and legislation to ensure the separation of powers (the *trias politica*).

The functionality of democracy also demands conscientious commitment to its basic principles: the intrinsic value of every person; respect for and fulfilment of human rights; just processes in decision-making and power use; and the common good as the goal and guiding light for political activity. If these principles are not commonly shared, democracy is in peril and will function deficiently.

There are many social institutions that are manifestations of the value base of democracy, human rights and the constitutional state. Their existence is not enough in itself, however. Giving grand speeches at the 150th anniversaries of those institutions will not reach those who doubt whether their existence is justified in the first place. The most valuable issues need defenders and defences that are linked to people's everyday lives. Immigrants coming from different cultural backgrounds, for example, may be well justified in mistrusting authorities and institutions.

Democracy involves freedom of values and opinions, and regard for diversity. Freedom of opinion, in all its variety, can only be fulfilled when commitment to the aforementioned principles is true. Many democracies are currently undergoing a phase in which freedom of opinion and expression is used as a weapon against democracy itself. The United States Capitol attack of January 2021 was not just an attack against the core of democracy by means of physical force, but also an attempt to undermine the very principles of democracy.

The ability to have one's say creates cohesion. This applies not only to political decisions but also to technological development. A democracy rooted in dialogue and thoughtful deliberation is the best medicine for collective trauma. Reforms must be designed from the perspective of those with the most to lose. It can help to prevent the appearance of collective trauma, and increase trust. Is it difficult? Yes. Time-consuming? Absolutely. But it is also durable. We cannot afford to make brittle reforms.

The operating model used by our public administration and lawmakers has been one of management by 'production and solutions'. The remit of the authorities has been to know the right answers and to implement solutions based on these. Public power has meant having authority to decide on the citizens' behalf. Every specific issue has its own expert or bureau, and the citizen is seen as a problem to solve. Annual budgeting, strategies and plans for each organisation, which lock the right answers for the future into place, worked during times of linear change but wobble significantly in our complex systemic reality. The separation between the different parts of the administration, and the partial optimisation that that leads to, makes overall service integration difficult to achieve. Even Max Weber (1864–1920) in his time described how bureaucracy can chain individuals into an impersonal iron cage of rational, rule-based control. The description is proving to be apt.

Our ways of processing joint issues and connecting to society must be improved to ensure that diverse opinions can be channelled into solutions. If a variety of opinions is not considered, people's commitment to developing the society will weaken. Ignored perspectives will simmer and sizzle until they reach boiling point.

Paradoxically, in today's circumstances, improving equality requires us to identify and react differently to different kinds of needs. At the same time, it facilitates a change and growth in ways of approaching challenges based on citizens' intrinsic motivations. This generates resilience and the functional ability of individuals and communities to process new situations. An empowering administration sees people and communities not as debts to be paid but as shared wealth to enjoy.

We Are Reimagining Governance for a Planetary Context

HOW CAN we make more room for diversity within the scope of jointly agreed rules of play? Debates have ended up on the axes of good/bad or right/wrong, when instead the focus should have been on jointly determining rules that create the necessary arena for pluralism. Those rules would apply to all members of the community, both "old" and "new".

Valuing variety and heterogeneity means creating a safe space for them. That is the most important supporting structure for pluralism. We need to find ways of integrating perspectives that may seem contradictory, for multi-perspectivity to be heard, seen and valued. But, in order to remain functional, we must have shared rules – a level of coherence that can foster growth and development in individuals, communities and the society as a whole. It is a question of setting limitations for growth and development with the purpose of supporting people's freedom and prosperity. Coherent diversity.

In an uncertain and diverse operating environment, it makes sense to relegate decision-making to the places that are experiencing the presumed problems, where the greatest motivation exists for solving them. Giving instructions without knowing the context is a shot in the dark. It is hard to give effective instructions for life to a person one has never met. Diversity is easier to understand in a location where people see eye to eye, on the same level, and all sides have opportunities to be heard.

The impact of a public service is not created in a bureau but in the location where the service meets the citizen. At that point, the service either materialises or not. Public services are generated in the interaction between official bodies, citizens and other agents. The people whose problems are most affected by the issues must be placed at the centre of service design: they have the best understanding and motivation for coming up with solutions. The problem at hand may have weakened their capacity to focus on finding solutions, so they will need support and assistance for designing them. In this case, assistance refers to well-meaning support for progressing in the direction determined by the people suffering from the problem – not knowing or setting goals on their behalf. The longer the chain of feedback out to the official bodies responsible, the longer the solution will take to appear, and the greater the risk of it being unviable in practice.

In the tug-of-war between the public and private sectors, the value of the civic society can go unnoticed, but it is in the civic society that public authority finds its *raison d'être* and democracy finds its foundations. The right of free individuals to utilise their abilities together to remodel the society must not be forgotten. Municipal councils, non-governmental organisations and local business enterprises contain a lot of exceptional thinking.

The state is needed to safeguard citizens against despotism and oppression. If the state is too strong, it will stifle people's freedoms; if it is too weak, it will lack the courage and trust to reach its full potential. We must strive to maintain the tension between the state and an open society, and to see it as a positive force. The state is not an end in itself, but a way of organising interactions between people that permit individuals and communities to prosper. The state is successful if its structures draw out the best in each of us and allow for the fulfilment of each of our individual and collective freedoms.

The challenge now is how we can begin to perceive relationships and interactions differently at a global scale in a situation already fraught with tension, polarised opinion, mental health burdens and extensive feelings of anger, fear and injustice.

Many of the societies that have flourished over time have collapsed at some point. Researchers have tried to find causes and identify similarities between the collapses. The historian Joseph Tainter has proposed that the civilisations in question developed to such levels of social, political and cultural complexity that their ability to respond to new emerging challenges was insufficient. The solutions to previous problems increased complexity, and in such a complex structure, the cost of new solutions ended up being greater than the benefit to be gained from them. Therefore, the society failed at integrating its isolated, specialised systems to a new, higher level. The complexity of the community's thinking and problem-solving ability was no match for the increased complexity of the operating environment, which meant that the civilisations in question ended up entrapped by their own success.

A significant part of the success of the human race is our ability to share attention with others. We learn from, in and with others, imitating and copying them. When someone finds a solution, it is quickly shared with others; this stops the society from regressing but, on the other hand, continuously increases complexity and its subsequent cost. Thanks to our accelerated and networked communication and logistics systems, our development is now intercultural and international.

Today's society is, in fact, global. Decisions made in individual nations no longer stay within the boundaries of those nations but have a broad impact in our mutually dependent world. The effects are not unidirectional, either: they link backwards, too. Computerised models of climate change clearly indicate this, as did the spread and evolution of new variants of the coronavirus.

Today's global citizens are increasingly highly educated and willing to move across borders. More and more people have the option of relocating in search of a better life. Some are forced to do so due to worsening living conditions and climatic impacts. Exploitation of natural resources and upholding international inequality will most often come back to bite the exploiter. Leaving societies that are tormented by poverty and conflict to their own devices until their states collapse will have consequences that we find in our own backyards – sooner than ever before.

We are interdependent in many ways. Unless we are able to rise jointly to a more complex, more integrated and higher level in our worldview, the civilisation's collapse will affect every person in the world. We have much more to lose than before.

Human behaviour has become the greatest threat to biodiversity, the planet's ecosystems and the availability of fresh water, air and soil. Changing our own human behaviours is the only sustainable way in which the long-lasting and ever-accelerating negative trend can be turned.

Therefore, we need structures and rules that facilitate this on a global level. And yet, antithetically, many of the global structures built after the Second World War have consciously been dismantled in recent years, or their legitimacy has been undermined. If ever there was a need for global rules, forums, tools and agreement practices, it is now. These will not arise without a global citizenship identity. We have many identities and they do not have to compete with each other. We are diverse, but our underlying identity, shared by all the people in the world, and the ensuing ethics must be reinforced.

Our social circles have expanded from family and tribal units to larger networks. Dunbar's Number, named after the anthropologist Robin Dunbar, suggests that 150 is the number of social relationships that an average person is able to maintain. Communities larger than that require norms and shared stabilising rules to function collectively. The development of nations is an example of that being possible. In the development of nations, a sense of unity has been created by national identity, which was not created overnight but over centuries.

For larger communities, such as the European Union, identity development is still under way. It remains to be seen whether we will ever be able to create a joint European identity and ethical responsibility by which German taxpayers, for example, are willing to pay for improving the quality of life of poorer people in Greece. The challenge of finding a shared identity and ethics on a global level is even greater – and yet, even more urgent. Do we feel responsible for each other and are we prepared to assist each other as global citizens?

Factually, we have spent a very short proportion of our human evolution cognisant of the limitations of the planet and of nature, and of the ensuing problems that require global coordination.

Therefore it is no wonder that the practical applications of global rules and shared ethics have not immediately succeeded. We must not be demoralised by this. This is the very learning and spiritual growth challenge that all of us global citizens face. It is one requiring collective transformation.

We Are the One and the Many

IN BIOPHYSICAL evolution, what was once one is multiplied. Yet even after multiplying, it still also remains one. This unity in diversity also applies to cultural evolution. Although cultures diverge and fragment, they are still based on unified oneness. That is the oneness and connection of humanity. We tend to forget this. The idea only comes up when faced with extreme circumstances. The oneness that connects all of us is the factor on which we can build our global identity.

We believe that we, as humans, protect nature. The situation is fundamentally the opposite: nature protects us. It protects us and our opportunities to live and prosper on the planet. Therefore we must defend nature and create economies, cultures and technologies that safeguard its diversity. Reciprocity is the basis for sustainable cohabitation, and we have not only the ethical imperative to maintain it, but also a selfish reason to do so.

You cannot negotiate with nature: the Covid pandemic was a good example of this. We couldn't ask the virus to slow down for a moment while we worked on improving our healthcare capacity and vaccines. The pandemic revealed how vulnerable the idea of humans as masters of the world actually is. We have tried to control nature, but that has effects that we cannot predict.

Climate change will not invite us to the negotiating table, either, when things get really bad. In labour disputes between people and organisations, we can mutually agree to stop the clocks to come up with a solution within a given time. With nature we can't do that: nature sets the pace. We have reached our global limits and must take the planetary perspective better into account. Hence we need a global identity to join our other identities. Nature must be brought to the core of economic activity, from the perspective of the planet's resilience. How can we create circumstances in which future generations have enough alternatives for living symbiotically with the environment?

In this respect, we have sown bad seeds for the next generation. They will have fewer alternatives than we do, and less time to learn and make decisions: a smaller window of opportunity, a narrower quality of life. We can still affect the seeds that will germinate into the coming generations' living environment, however. We can turn the wheel on current developments and set the course; create dependencies on a better path – a path that does not lead to the destruction of species, including our own, but to recovery of diversity and a greater window of opportunity for future generations.

None of us can choose our birth culture, gender, ethnicity or skin colour in advance. The perspective we grow into, from which we view the world, has a great impact, however. Each culture has stories that present knowledge in their own ways. The stories make marks that we cannot shed even if we rebel against them, because even then we will be defined by them. Once again our ability for perspectival knowledge is emphasised: we must learn to put ourselves in the shoes of an Ethiopian girl, a Bangladeshi farmer or a Yemeni teacher. Any of us could have been born into their realities. How does that make us feel about Western welfare or global justice?

The philosopher John Rawls has provided a tool for thinking and acting according to global identity and ethics. His idea of the "veil of ignorance" refers to people agreeing on joint moral norms in such a way that those agreeing have no way of knowing which position they will end up in themselves. Global justice can only spring from those who hold the responsibility for global shared decisions being cognisant of this. If we are prepared to accept solutions without knowing our own fates, we will be making decisions that strive for the common good. In this way, we will grant the highest level of freedom to each person that does not limit the freedoms of other people, and we will only accept financial inequality to the extent that it will maximally benefit those left in the worst positions.

Reducing inequality and poverty requires a shift in our way of seeing others as global citizens. The goals of sustainable development are interdependent: they cannot be solved one by one but have to be worked on as a whole.

Apocalyptic fear mongering is not an effective way to motivate people to change their ways. Nor is it realistic to tell people to give up their current livelihoods and live more ethically, even though they'll have nothing to live on. This is why we must find ways of changing systems that incentivise people to live more sustainably. Instead of obligation, it must be based on intrinsic motivation. That, in turn, requires a building of trust.

Multi-year initiatives have been put in place to restore fish stocks in the Gulf of Mexico, with a starting point in reinforcing the resilience of individual fishing communities in the area. The first action was to build a football field for the village children. The project managers moved into the village. Decisions on the measures to implement always remain in the hands of the community and its fishers. It has been necessary to prove that there are alternative ways of making a living besides fishing; learning about agriculture and personally experiencing what it meant to receive an income from farming led to the fishing community deciding to limit fishing while fish stocks recover. At the same time, they set limits and rules for the point at which it would be permissible to return to fishing, and at what volumes. The journey from building the football field to fish stocks recovering took time but also proved that sustainable change is possible.

The competitiveness of nations must not be seen as a zero-sum game. If developed nations only view Africa as a continent of exploitable resources, the result will be unsustainable living conditions causing an uncontrollable wave of migration, whose cost will be astronomical for everyone. That is not sustainable from anyone's point of view.

Politics and economics are crucial products of our civilisation that allow us to take care of shared issues, organise interaction and improve prosperity, well-being and quality of life. The purpose of the economy is to increase prosperity and the size of the cake that we all share; the purpose of politics is to ensure that the cake is divided fairly. Both have forgotten their purposes and ended up as prisoners of their means.

The shared cake and prosperity have become synonyms of wealth: of how individuals can make more money for themselves. The economy optimises gain; politics optimises power. Both of them focus on the short term, the economy on quarterly results and politics on electoral periods. The agglomeration of wealth and power is measured within those time scales. The purposes of both systems should be rediscovered.

To survive, we must optimise prosperity – the joint prosperity of people and nature. We must harness the positive incentives of the market economy to achieve this. Similarly, politicians must understand that unless we shed the obsession with power and conflict, the unwritten rules of politics will become an obstacle.

Human activity has become the main force affecting our planet and we can use it for our own benefit or detriment. Committing to a global ethical identity is the next step, and it should have happened before we committed to a global economy.

I would like to have been a fly on the wall, back when there were no flies or walls.

We fail to read the message of the empty space.

We believe that we, as humans, protect nature. The situation is fundamentally the opposite: nature protects us.

Instead of carefully defining what each member of the organisation should do, it is more important to determine what no one should be doing.

"Being yourself" doesn't work by yourself.

It is a perspective shift from solving problems to developing the system.

Tomorrow morning, when you squeeze your stripy toothpaste onto your brush, consider how it got there.

Climate change will not invite us to the negotiating table when things get really bad.

Part Four: Pathways

Q: So now what do we do?

A: Learn! Learning is an emergent property of purposive social interaction. We need to learn who we are – a collective journey into ourselves – with this view of learning in mind. A tangible proposition to build a planetary ethos through education is outlined.

1. *Learning as Adaptive Advantage*
2. *Learning as Prefigurative Culture*
3. *Learning as Relating*
4. *Learning as Predicting the Unpredictable*
5. *Learning as Collective Development*
6. *Learning as Dialogue*
7. *Learning as Autonomy and Trust*
8. *Learning as Self-direction*
9. *Learning as Leadership*
10. *Learning as Universal Imperative*
11. *Learning as Global Ethic*
12. *Learning as a Journey into Ourselves*

Learning as Adaptive Advantage

WE ARE altering our environment more quickly than we are able to prepare ourselves for the alterations. This asynchronism between the exponential rate of cultural revolution and the development of our biological abilities is becoming extreme. We can alter our mindsets and adopt new psychotechnologies to support our inner worlds; we can reform social structures through human interaction, and reconstruct the physical frameworks of our societies, for instance in the form of institutions and logistical systems. But we cannot alter human biology. Biology sets limitations, and although we change in interaction with our environment, our ability to evolve is asymmetrical. The way in which our brains react to threats evolved in completely different surroundings from our current ones. The rate at which biological changes take place is significantly slower than that of the human mind, social relationships or physical structures. Natural selection's mutations are too slow at helping us adapt to changes in the environment.

However, we humans have evolved one property that does not include ready-made solutions pre-programmed into our DNA, but happens in real time and in interaction with our environment: *learning*. This ability is more advanced in us than in other species, and that is what allows us to adapt so well to different circumstances. Natural selection has favoured our ever-emerging learning ability.

In the grip of the ten illusions that I have laid out above, our learning ability has never been more crucial, but not only incrementally within our current frames: it must be transformational if it is to enable us to step outside of our illusory frames.

Transformation is often seen as a sudden one-off event – metamorphosis in a few seconds from caterpillar to butterfly, from water to ice or from villain to hero. Our sceptical minds suspect that this can only happen in nature and the movies, but not in our own lives. Indeed, in human life, transformation is often slow and sometimes unnoticeable – a gradual growth through the interplay of the conscious and subconscious. The possibility of transformation lies in all of us, and conscious self-knowledge and reflection on mindsets are steps in fulfilling that possibility. It is about viewing the world differently so that the world that we view also changes. All the complexity, uncertainty and unsafety of the world lie in us. By going through it, joining the dots of reality into an understandable picture, we can reach a new level of clarity.

However, this is not an individual sport. Learning is an emerging quality of a social system. It enables the system to develop according to its purposes and needs. The emerging qualities of a system are not as permanent as its physical ones; they must continuously be maintained and reinforced to stop them from deteriorating.

Circumstances that are favourable for learning at the individual, societal, organisational and national levels, invite curiosity and ignorance as resources, not as causes for shame. They do not succumb to viewing success as a permanent state of being. Human diversity is a strength because it implies considerations and views from more perspectives. Opinions and open dialogue should be encouraged, and because the road to learning passes through failure, psychological safety and trust are indispensable. There should be no room for fear.

Learning is often seen as big business for the future, but it must not be reduced to a transactional service between provider and user. Learning is a deeply ethical process of being and becoming human. It can raise us out of the bog of instrumental thinking and gain-seeking, onto the firmer ground of different values and worldviews. At the heart of progress lies the question of how we treat each other, to what extent we value and care for each other. Learning can lead us onto the path of collective wisdom.

Learning as Prefigurative Culture

LEARNING IS a large investment – not in monetary terms, but in terms of the personal resources we must assign to it. Our brain is a kind of Keeper of the Privy Purse, allocating resources based on where it considers them to be most necessary. Its budget comprises not money but the neurotransmitters, hormones and energy that are essential for regulating our vital functions. The biggest investments our body makes are into moving itself and learning new things. Traversing familiar ground is a smaller investment than moving into unknown territory. Learning is the most expensive thing a person can undertake, but it is justified by the idea that the investment will pay for itself in time.

Michael Tomasello, Co-Director of the Max Planck Institute for Evolutionary Anthropology, has researched the ways in which apes and human children learn and adopt social skills. He says that collective 'cultural' learning is a skill specific to humans (Tomasello, 2016). It is an evolutionary step forward from ape interaction, which is based on competition. Humans are characterised by our ability to teach others – stopping to see the same thing or event from another's perspective and consciously using exaggerated imitation, drawing the other person's attention to external factors and repeatedly attempting to read their mind to find out what they know. Teaching requires mutual trust in potential success, the ability to perceive the learner's starting points in knowledge and competence, and the ambition to do one's best to achieve quality learning. The focusing of communal attention and target orientation are human strengths. We should learn to optimise our use of these and minimise the erroneous or self-destructive aspects that they involve.

The cultural anthropologist Margaret Mead (1970) divided societies into three categories, depending on how they conducted the transfer of cultural heritage to coming generations. She called them postfigurative, cofigurative and prefigurative cultures.

In the first category, the older generation claims to know what knowledge and skills the next generation will need. In static cultures that experienced few alterations, generations could pass on their operating models, rituals and competences nearly unchanged. What was once learnt, was passed on from father to son and mother to daughter.

In the second category, the older generation had to strive to predict the new skills and abilities that their successors might need. They were aware that the coming generation would encounter new challenges, but felt that they could predict them in a way that allowed them to pass on at least the "correct answers" as to what abilities would be needed.

In the third category, changes are multiple and they happen quickly. The preceding generation understands that this unpredictability means that they cannot know what challenges, work tasks or knowledge the younger generations will encounter. It is not enough to transfer heritage; they must provide their descendants with skills to cope with uncertainty and ambiguity, to create their own futures, to learn to learn, and to maintain functional ability through crises, as well as self-reflection and self-knowledge to reinforce their agency. The ability to read a context in flux becomes essential, making improvisation a wise kind of spontaneity.

In many parts of the world, cultural accumulation has progressed so far, through networking and mutual dependence, that we have reached the third category of prefigurative culture. Great steps forward are needed in the ways in which we prepare the next generation for the future. Providing ready-made answers and knowledge is not enough. Making ethically sustainable choices is not possible by memorising generally applicable ethical rules; decisions must be made on a case-by-case basis. It is best to focus on building abilities and capacities, attitudes and values that are needed when one encounters new, unpredicted and uncertain situations, and when one wants to make ethically and aesthetically sustainable choices.

It is to this quandary that all education systems are currently seeking answers. How much knowledge and how many skills? The alteration has been ongoing and discernible for several decades already, but the need for action is growing every day. The amount of content to teach has been increased for so long that curricula are filled to the brim and are overwhelming for teachers and students alike. The amount of time that can be spent in school is limited, so choices have to be made. Broad skills in learning, descriptions of learner profiles, various thinking methods and learning compass models among many others can help in reinforcing the ability of children and adolescents to build their own futures.

Learning as Relating

WE HUMANS can read each other's thoughts. We do it all the time: we search for familiar patterns, previous similar situations, clues in facial expressions and body language. We ponder different alternatives and consider their consistency and likelihood at lightning speed, without realising what we are actually doing. Unlike humans, in many apes the sclera of the eye – the part that on humans is white – is dark, which makes it hard to tell what they are looking at. Some say that the ability to read another person's intentions in their eyes was so crucial to human survival that we evolved to have white sclera. That is why it sometimes bothers us if the person we are talking to is wearing sunglasses.

Mirror neurons are tasked with mirroring what other people do, and how that feels. They link us to each other and our feelings. We have 43 facial muscles that are trained to reveal or conceal our feelings, thoughts and desires. We are deeply social beings.

In their book *The Enigma of Reason: A New Theory of Human Understanding*, Hugo Mercier and Dan Sperber (2017) suggest that the basis for the evolution of reason is found in sociability. For them, reasoning is not a process of finding optimal solutions but one of justifying and rationalising our actions and opinions to others. It is us doing a sort of internal "dry run" of situations where someone questions why we acted as we did.

In human collaborations, reasoned justifications are crucial messages. When we reveal our reasoning, we are communicating how we intend to act in similar, future situations. As children, we have games as a way of practising and learning how people behave in real-life situations. Even children are capable of working out who can be trusted in each situation.

Reputation is a major factor affecting our argumentation. Why do we lie? Why is it so difficult to be wrong? We are driven by a desire to look good before others. We hide many things that go on in our minds, protecting our inner selves. We grow shields that defend us but also limit our growth. Feelings of anger and shame often cover up a fear arising from our true needs, which we want to hide because revealing them would make us vulnerable. Impossible to hide perfectly, they bubble up to the surface as bursts of irritation or rage.

In his day, the economist John Maynard Keynes (1936) said, "It is astonishing what foolish things one can temporarily believe if one thinks too long alone." We need interaction to correct our thought biases. While others' mistakes are easy to see, we fail to notice our own.

Because reason is so significant socially, it is essential to pay attention to the kind of value group that we inhabit. Research has shown that we form opinions and absorb information that demonstrates our loyalty to the community with which we identify (Clifford, 2017). We have a herd mentality.

You can test this theory by considering whether you associate negative qualities with people who think differently. Can you trust a vegan? Are Muslims somehow 'other' Are a specific party's voters somehow weird?

Learning is an activity that takes place interactively. We have at least four major interactive relationships: with ourselves; with other people; with our created mental and physical culture; and with nature. Each of us is on a learning and growth journey to the conscious appreciation of being human.

Learning as Predicting the Unpredictable

How does learning work? According to Stanislas Dehaene (2020), "to learn is to form an internal model of the external world." The brain contains thousands of predictive models of the world it inhabits, which means that it merges our inner and outer worlds, our physical and mental realities. We are continuously trying to resolve the tensions between our predictions and the sensory data we are experiencing.

One way of seeking cohesion between our inner and outer worlds is to alter the outer one: we have been extremely efficient at this, especially of late. The more we alter the environment – the forum of our agency – the less we can rely on the biological heritage we have evolved over millions of years: the algorithm of natural selection. The "factory settings" of evolution and the competence and qualities given to us at birth are an increasing mismatch for the demands for adaptation of the environment, i.e. our context-dependent "custom settings". For example, this is why we struggle so much with rapid multitasking, why the endless pop-ups and tempting links of the internet keep us in their grasp, and why obesity has become a global phenomenon. When the diversity of our surroundings increases quickly, the tension between our biological and cultural evolution is heightened.

The other way of finding resolution between our inner and outer worlds is to refine our inner sensing. Humans are sensorimotor entities: our senses and movements are strongly linked, forming a feedback loop of mutual learning. Movement is a way for us to exist and to act in our environment. Thoughts form the feedback channels between our sensory and motor functions. If we move in ways that cause us harm, it is essential for our survival to learn to rethink them. Say we move in a specific terrain and receive a near-fatal snake bite; it makes sense to consider whether that terrain is one we should revisit. Thinking allows us to make informed choices. Instead of the snake snuffing us out, we can snuff out the thought of going to the place that is rife with snakes.

The uncertainty of our global predicaments demand an ethical, deep and radical readiness to think differently, altering our default mindsets. I don't mean the kind of radical change as that achieved by violent revolutions; I mean the self-correcting renewal that takes place through a reinforcement of our human self-knowledge and responsibility. This requires an increase in individual self-reflection, as well as new tools and forums for sowing the seeds of collective wisdom.

Updating our enlightenment mission is one response to the new pressures of coping with uncertainty. The Enlightenment brought us knowledge, science and education, to add certainty to reality. We can see today that despite our progress, its mission has not entirely been fulfilled. We are beset by anxiety at the unpredictability. Therefore we must update our enlightenment mission to provide us with the ability to understand and utilise our first-, second- and third-person perspectives.

The first-person perspective entails conscious presence as a human, self-knowledge and the ability to connect with external reality – to hum in the same key while creating new things as part of our surroundings. Understanding our thought and perception biases is essential to our ability to utilise this perspective. The first person adds an empirical point of view to reality.

The second-person perspective refers to our ability to act and create new things in interaction, understanding what it means to be someone else or different, and making compromises to find sustainable solutions and value choices. Emotional and interactive abilities are essential. The second person contributes the experience of multi-perspectivity.

The third-person perspective looks at the world with the help of objective facts, generating, valuing and utilising scientific findings. It emphasises critical thought and information literacy. The third person contributes factual, scientific truths to our ways of seeing reality.

None of these perspectives is enough by itself. We must find ways to integrate them whenever we are handling individual, local, national or global problems. It is not an easy goal, because the perspectives involve incompatibilities and tensions. Coping with uncertainty and ambiguity demands an increase in mental and cognitive flexibility.

Learning as Collective Development

DISCUSSIONS ON how to make the world a better place have no political sex appeal. Voters and the media want answers to questions beginning with "what", and on those the politicians feverishly concentrate: what savings, what legislation, what taxes to raise or to lower. If we focused on the question of "how", we would be forced to consider whether we are doing the right things: How can we best increase our citizens' experiences of well-being? How can we reinforce the resilience of local communities and schools?

More attention should be paid to *how* we can enhance our way of fulfilling set targets. It does not have to be a zero-sum game, a power struggle or a reshuffling of boxes. Operating models can be found that increase power and empowerment from everyone's perspective. It requires overhauling our thinking, from today's hierarchical, control-based governance towards collective development. More than anything, it requires belief in people's own ability and motivation to take better responsibility, given the opportunity. That will not happen in an instant, because the current biases are so deeply rooted in our roles and expectations. And yet, it would appear to be rather urgent.

I hear my former politician self, asking whether an election can be won going down that route. Maybe, maybe not. It depends on one's ability to justify the importance of the change.

1. We need a collective process for creating a picture of how things currently stand. Such a situational picture of reality is fundamental if we are to form diverse views on what we would like it to be. We need a shared concept of reality, otherwise we cannot work together.
2. We must boost our ability to imagine possible futures on the local and global levels. Shedding our path-dependence requires this ability.
3. We must create a trusted process of merging diverse perspectives and value bases into one desired direction in which we want to move. The main thing is to have a collective process that is acceptable for everyone – including those whose perspectives are ultimately not included in the decisions. Individuals must have as much freedom as possible to live according to their worldviews and values, to the extent that they do not infringe on others' freedom to do the same.
4. We must find an operating model for people with different points of view and motivations to strengthen their agency, such that individuals' spiritual growth is coupled with global sustainability in the best interests of people and the planet alike.

The birth of the scientific worldview and the progress that has been experienced in academia in the last couple of centuries have provided us with significant new tools for understanding reality. Scientific methods are used for providing empirical evidence of how things stand. What was previously thought of as common sense has often been proven wrong. Meanwhile, the humanities have shed light on *why* things are as they are.

To have the ability to live in safety and prosperity in this uncertain time, we must start to raise from the shadows some of the forgotten ways of looking at the world and processing information. To relinquish our lopsided way of looking at reality and its illusions, I believe it is time to pay attention to capabilities such as creating and understanding the big picture and fathoming the interactions therein; relating events and actions to their contexts; meeting the new and uncertain things that are constantly engendered in our complex world and seeing the new opportunities that emerge; using intuition and imagination and being prepared to wonder at things; experiencing nonverbally, sensing the connections between body and mind, and valuing tacit, personal knowledge; recognising emotions, nuances and uniqueness; thinking about our own thinking and realising the extent of our ignorance. These capabilities must be woven more closely into our processes of collective understanding.

Possessing a broader and more comprehensive situational picture helps us make better decisions. The ability to combine the verbal and nonverbal, the exact and inexact, the measurable and immeasurable – those are some of the requirements for our new etiquette to be created. A broader scope of vision also requires the engendering of new roles: "coordinators of knowledge bases", "bridge-builders of worldviews", "tolerators and tolerance-enhancers of uncertainty", and "overseers of multi-perspectivity".

It is always worth pausing at any tension found between one's opinion and scientific data. Research results and views that conflict with our beliefs should be of interest to us. In issues that we find particularly confusing, it is worth acquainting ourselves with the views of the highest experts – even if they disagree between themselves – and try to understand their ways of thinking.

After that, it is time to think for ourselves.

Learning as Dialogue

WE SEE what we know – and vice versa. Swiftly deepening specialisation and delegation of tasks based on expertise are society's ways of solving problems. Professional expertise is like a spotlight that helps you see what is lit in clear detail. But light also creates shadow; it leaves things outside of it. Expertise enlightens *and* blinds us.

An *amateur*, from the Latin word for lover (*amator*), is a person who loves what they do. An amateur lacks formal training and qualifications – those famous glasses that come with the lenses prescribed by expertise. Wearing the glasses, a professional can see things that the amateur misses. On the other hand, the glasses make reality look different for the professional than for the rest of us. Therefore, an amateur will sometimes see things missed by the professional.

"Give a small boy a hammer, and he will find that everything he encounters needs pounding," said Abraham Kaplan. It must have been a boy over the age of five, because research has shown that children younger than that lack that kind of functional attachment to assigning a single purpose for a tool. The idea makes me chuckle. There are all too many situations where we rush in, grasping the hammer of our professional expertise, and start pounding the nails of the correct answers to the problem. I have sometimes blistered my hands with all the hammering.

"These days they start too much from the structure of the organisation, thinking about which box this or that family's problems belong in," said a young person in the paper about their experiences with child welfare services (*Helsingin Sanomat*, 6 April 2018). People, communities and societies are all multifarious entities, and wearing the glasses of deep specialisation can prevent someone from seeing them as a whole. Often, solving problems related to people requires the person's own commitment and participation. An expert's analysis and solution are only half-finished if the customer is isolated as an object without agency. The solution may even be detrimental if it is blind to the big picture. We receive a diagnosis when what we need is a dialogue.

Despite their unpleasantness, the early days of the Covid-19 pandemic gave us a lot of valuable information about this kind of dialogue in the face of the unknown. People's lives were threatened by an invisible and largely unknown peril. The motivation to acquire information for survival was at its peak: curiosity is too mild a term to describe our thirst for information at that time. What was particularly interesting was people's ways of figuring out what was going on. We turned to each other in many ways. Experts played a significant role, as research institutions shared a lot of their findings and data, but so too did individuals, as they shared experiences in their neighbourhoods and on social media and quickly crowdsourced diverse protective methods. Heads of nations consulted each other to learn from and copy good political practices. I do not recall a time when national education systems – which are usually proudly self-sufficient – have worked together so swiftly to align their decisions.

Learning is possible when we encounter new things. The new is often frightening, and that can make us fall into the trap of reactive learning. Reactive learning refers to acting in the same ways again and again: for example, repeating in our family lives the models we witnessed in our childhood. If the schools we attended were based on reactive learning, why should we behave differently after leaving school? Despite experiencing changes, we repeat former models of action: we do the same things as before, even though perhaps better in the new situation. As Russell Ackoff (2010) has said, "Almost every major social problem that confronts us today is a consequence of trying to do the wrong things righter." We cannot shed the habitual patterns, even though our circumstances differ.

Learning can be more than that. Deeper learning is facilitated by interaction between thinking and doing, self-knowledge and a connection between the self and the dynamically changing reality. What we learn becomes a part of our identity. Internal growth – what we could call edification, civilisation or culture – becomes possible. All of those concepts include the idea of applying the fruits of growth for the good of the community.

The hardest thing is to remove one's professional glasses and look at the profession with an outsider's eyes. Coming up with sustainable solutions requires adapting one's thinking to the complexity of the problems at hand. The smaller the blind spot of expertise that they cannot self-reflect on, the better the expert.

Each of us is an expert at being ourselves. That also involves light and shadow. When we gain the ability to look at our glasses and change the lenses as necessary, we learn to cope better in a complex world. We will have greater freedom to see the world. That is not a bad objective.

Many examples exist of situations where experts in their fields listen to each other and work together. An accomplished jazz band is a perfect manifestation of this. When the band gets together, they tune their instruments so they can play together, and tune their minds to the mental landscape of the music to be performed. They start off with a shared motif that is known to all the players. After that, room is made for each player's solo – their own narrative on the motif. The other players support them and help each soloist succeed in telling their story. Because they are improvising, this support requires careful listening and reacting to aural cues. The players take inspiration from each other and develop the story further.

The most important parts of the performance happen in the interaction between the players, and the result is always unique. An experimental approach is permitted, and every failure is a new opportunity. As jazz legend Miles Davis put it: "If you hit a wrong note, it's the next note that you play that determines if it's good or bad." Although improvisation is a spontaneous creation, it is based on years of practice, preparation and finding one's voice. The audience and the rest of the context also direct the performance.

Improvising gives every soloist in turn a great freedom of expression. Far from ignoring others, however, this freedom means sensitively feeding the interaction with them. The commitment to the few shared rules must be completely internalised. Complete strangers can jam together and still come up with a functioning ensemble. Each player is one part of a whole, and their interaction is of the essence. The whole really is greater than the sum of its parts.

A jazz-like approach would also be valuable in other aspects of life today. More of us than ever are engaged with creating something as part of our work, while routine tasks are taken care of by machines and software. More than ever, we also have to work together to solve problems. Being human is a team effort. Unlike the conveyor belts of old, the work environment no longer stays the same day after day.

In dialogue, it is essential to be tuned to a shared frequency. Similarly, it involves appreciation and respect for the other parties in the dialogue as humans – not just as holders of specific roles. The participants are equal: no one is right or wrong. The main thing is to listen and to hear. We do not want everyone to improvise in the same way: just hearing different points of view is an end in itself.

The result we seek is not consensus but better understanding of different people's situations, motivations and perspectives. Surprisingly often, one will find that when the parties to a dialogue are freed from the demand of coming up with a shared opinion, they will find consensus anyway. The situation must feel safe and trust-cultivating for every participant. Also, everyone must be aware of and respect the process.

Dialogue is crucial for learning, because it allows every person the opportunity to examine their own frames and worldviews. We need each other to free us from the prisons of our perspectives. For dialogue to take place, we must give up the attitude of trying to convince others of our opinions. It is not a battle for victory between arguments but a step away from the war altogether, into peace. Having different opinions, and tension between them, is a good thing. That connects diversity to the oneness that lies beneath all the different perspectives.

Most groups and forums are committed to achieving or promoting a specific objective. Communities of unity and dialogue do not arise in our cult of short-term efficiency. I presume many will agree that it feels good just to spend time with people, without any performance targets. Meaning is born out of encounters and togetherness, being with others. There must be room for that. These kinds of encounters have been eliminated by our daily life of schedules and accomplishment. We need communities and groups with no purpose other than being together: no competition, no performance targets and no strategic utilisation of people for achieving a specific goal; just the opportunity to get together, spend time, listen, speak and connect to a shared silence.

When we admit our humanity, we open the gates of interaction. We cannot relate to perfect people, because perfect people do not exist, and we prefer not to open our hearts to dishonesty. We all suffer in this life and that makes us equals. We connect to each other in our vulnerability, because it gives us something familiar and meaningful to relate to.

Instead of focusing on individuals, all human activities should place the quality of interaction at the forefront. How can we create situations and circumstances where the quality of interaction is such that it allows for differences of opinion, the richness of diversity, the seeking of shared foundations and living in uncertainty?

Learning as Autonomy and Trust

THE FINNISH expression for "who wears the trousers in the house" is "who decides where the cupboard stands". Picture this: in the middle of a room stands an armoire, and two people disagree on the corner where it should stand. Both of them are stubbornly holding onto their opinions and start pushing the armoire towards the desired corner. They push and push, sweat running down their faces, but the armoire remains in the middle of the room. The result is a compromise, but neither person is happy – and the armoire can't stay in the middle of the room either.

How does this relate to our world and its shared decision-making? Say the armoire is a country's economy, or a social security reform. There are not two but dozens of people pushing it in different directions. The armoire circles around the room, as the number of pushers varies. The pushers make tactical public statements, trying to influence the others' actions and opinions concerning their own success. Looking from the doorway, nothing ever seems to be finished and one can lose faith in a result ever being reached. Having watched the hullabaloo for a while, one of the pushers decides to become a strong leader. They put a stop to the pushing and decide where the others should place the armoire – and by when. What happens?

Once the strongest leader's will is known, the others will proportion their actions to that. Some consider the decision to serve their own interests, while others drum up support to oppose the new direction. Because a timeline has been set, some go out of their way to build obstacles to prevent the schedule from being met, or cause delays for the same reason. Thus the strong leader's role turns against itself, causing a power struggle and controversy.

Another tactic is to predict the direction the armoire might take and then publicly announce support for that direction. It is easy to be on the winner's side.

In a hierarchy, getting the armoire to the desired corner is simple. The other participants submit to the leader's authority, so when the leader declares the direction, the others push accordingly. It is what some wish for in their nostalgia for bygone times, but that is not how the world works anymore. Individual decision-makers have less power than people generally believe. We have wanted to change society. Our lives are now networked. Power does not lie with individuals but in the relationships between people and decision-making bodies. When each one holds their own without yielding, the armoire dances around the room. And yet, everyone feels it is necessary, or else voters, paying members or lobby groups will withdraw their support.

The logic of a network is to some extent the opposite of a hierarchy. In the latter, those further down the ladder adapt their behaviour to match the wishes and opinions of those higher up. In the former, each agent draws attention to how their wishes and opinions differ from others'. In a hierarchy, the agents are known; in a network, new agents appear while old ones may withdraw, possibly to reappear later. In a hierarchy, goals have schedules, managers and process plans from start to finish. In a network, various agents work strategically from their own perspectives, which means that different parties will have different views on the goals, processes and schedules. A hierarchy plays on a limited playing field according to known rules, whereas a network's playing field is an amoebic, living thing whose rules are purposefully modified.

The quality of interactions and the trust that feeds this are vital for any desired changes to be completed in a networked and systemic environment. Trust is built out of reliability, credibility and closeness: reliability meaning keeping promises; credibility being the ability and competence to take care of one's appointed tasks; and closeness being the awareness and mutual knowledge of diverse autonomous agents, until they mutually understand each other's challenges and actions.

Reinforcing the agents' autonomy does not mean everybody being allowed to do what they feel like, without caring about others. On the contrary, extensive autonomy requires connecting to other agents in a jointly created, broad system. Like the jazz band, the players have a lot of freedom and therefore must have a special sensitivity to the others' playing for the result to be a good experience.

Shared learning works on the same logic, whether the interaction scale is that of individuals, communities, nations or the globe. The broader the whole, the more difficult it becomes, because then one must take into account the internal logic of subsystems, and how they are linked to the whole. One must understand that it has many levels and perspectives, and that various agents have different responsibilities. The agents in an extensive system always have particular responsibility for maintaining trust, as well as process responsibility for the functioning of the system.

A system is by nature collectively directed, because the essential developments occur due to or thanks to interaction. Because the context of a complex system is always changing, autonomous members must adapt to the evolving situation together. Self-directedness, understood as emphasising each individual's and group's independent actions, separate from others, works poorly. The complexity of managing such a system arises from the fact that no individual agent has the ability to handle wicked, complex problems by themselves. Only by working together can they go in the desired direction.

Working together also means involving the people who have traditionally been considered objects – those for whom the services or solutions are created. Functioning results cannot be achieved without giving them ownership and a chance to be heard.

Processing complex social problems requires the system to change from within. This, in turn, requires simultaneous renewal from and on many levels. One could call it portfolio learning, consisting of a number of mutually linked interventions that continually learn from each other.

In recent decades, it has been found around the world that large-scale social reforms have been more successful when they are implemented diversely through several mutually supportive interventions that learn from each other. Legislative reforms, strong commitment from decision-makers, use of market mechanisms, consumer behaviour, the society's value and attitude shifts and practical trials and developments all move in the same direction. This lays the necessary ground for system renewal and the system can seek a new, more optimal form within the enabling limitations set for it.

The Finnish education system is considered to be one of the best in the world. Some of the oft-mentioned factors behind this are highly trained teachers, support from the community for schools and teachers, egalitarian local schools and a culture that appreciates learning. These are all important factors and they are woven together by the fact that, thanks to the high level of learning within it, the Finnish education system is a network of autonomous agents with a strong foundation of trust and functioning interaction between diverse roles. The framework for operations and the main teaching and learning targets are set on the national level. The municipal (local authority) level is responsible for local curricula and for maintaining schools. The school and teachers themselves possess a high level of autonomy based on expertise, when it comes to pedagogical solutions and development.

Trust is also extended to students, who are not pressured by standardised testing, long days or jam-packed schedules. Instead room is left for growth and extracurricular life according to the child's development level. Finland has some of the lowest amounts of standardised exams, annual lessons and homework in OECD countries, and yet (or perhaps therefore) produces some of the highest learning outcomes.

According to the Finnish Basic Education Act, the main objective of primary and secondary education is "to support pupils' growth into humanity and into ethically responsible membership of society." The trust-reliant operating model has been created to support this objective. The Finnish schooling model is a representation of the empowering impact of autonomy and trust, which can continue to respond even as the contexts change around us. Rigid complacency about what once worked will not serve us, but the willingness to continually renew is vital.

The deeper renewal now necessary springs from the spheres of being and identity. It is slower and requires an active and positive attitude from everyone involved. For renewal to happen, we must make way for emotions, experiences, dreams, assumptions, values and attitudes to rise to the surface. Because renewal always involves giving something up, time and space must also be given for grieving.

Learning as Self-direction

CHANGES IN our mental framings are strongly linked to action. Humans are psychophysical entities, and almost all our activities are based on the body's movements. When we notice something, we turn our heads towards it while mentally processing what we have perceived. At the same time, the thoughts generated by our perceptions make us move in a certain direction. We often view change as thinking about something in order to reach a conclusion and then acting accordingly. The flow also goes the other way: action will alert us to a cognitive conflict, which leads us to changing our mindset. In this way, action has led to a change in humanity and identity-development.

We can also do more things than we are able to describe verbally. Our actions manifest knowledge that we might not even know we possess. Elderly people may not recollect or be able to describe what they did when their children were babies, but put a grandchild in their laps and they will realise how much they know.

A good way to alter our perceptions through action is experimentation. It is wise to try things out if you don't know what you should do to achieve positive development, or what will happen if you implement a plan. True experimentation involves the understanding that there is no such thing as failure: all outcomes are valuable because they provide valuable information. Productive learning always takes place through mistakes. We must anticipate risks and minimise the kinds of mistakes that can lead to their realisation. The culture of experimentation is not in discord with this. We must have room to learn from our mistakes, and this can only happen through a culture of psychological safety and trust.

If a mistake leads to searching for culprits and punishment, we are on the wrong road, because it will actually cause lying, concealment, shame and fear. All of these are toxic to learning from mistakes. They may result in guilty parties being identified and brought to shame, but the causes behind the mistake are not processed because the dramatic arc ends with apportioning blame. The veil of forgetting completes the anatomy of the journey, which then continues towards an unimaginative and fearful reality of repeating the same mistakes.

Most people welcome opportunities to experiment and create in their own work. Beneath the surface, every community has a considerable mass of factors, including status and relationship patterns, unofficial organisations, cultures and unspoken taboos, which have built up over the years. In a society, the mass beneath the surface also includes shared experiences and traumas, prejudices, myths, folklore and archetypes.

The individual's ability to possess agency in such a context is critical in light of our unpredictable and uncertain future. Knowledge and skills are important, but what we are willing and capable of doing with them is even more consequential. Our growth into self-directedness should therefore be emphasised, and at its heart lie our ability to think about our thinking, explore our emotions and consider our mindsets. It is also the main element on the road to wisdom. It opens the fifth level of Robert Kegan's (1995) development model: the "self-transforming mind", i.e. the ability to transform together with our surroundings.

But supporting such self-directedness is difficult. In a child's development, a teacher or other adult is needed to detect the child's gradual and age-appropriate growth in taking care of themselves, their own learning and the fulfilment of their goals. Self-directedness is challenging even for adults – especially if our close circle, community or work organisation is founded on an old-fashioned culture of orders and direction coming from above. Over time, such a hierarchical culture becomes a kind of security blanket, because it is familiar. Moving on to make decisions on one's own life and work can then feel unsafe and unpleasant. Growing into self-directedness, autonomy and collectivity requires time, as well as opportunities for the necessary reflection.

Learning as Leadership

THE LEADER'S identity and role is undergoing major changes, hatching from the old shell of pinstripe suits and hierarchical thinking. Leadership and leaders are still needed in our changing environment, but their roles and identities are very different from before. Leadership as a word makes us think of the individual – the leader and their attributes. Leadership can, however, also be understood as the process in which collective decision-making takes place.

The main question then becomes how to create better methods for that process. How can we generate a collective process that accepts that making decisions is not a competition where one wins and the other loses, but an infinite game that continuously evolves, whose aim is to have as many players as possible?

The idea of control lives on strongly in organisations and their management. Yearning for a strong leader and belief in the cascading strategy are still realities in many organisations. The ideal of the heroic leader is hard to erase.

While demand for services and products is becoming diversified and changes continuously through systemic interaction, agents whose only goal is organisational efficiency grow blind, deaf and unable to adjust. The leader will sail a super-efficient ship on a sea of meaninglessness. In a complex operating environment, an organisation's operations should be built from the outside in, with the needs of the customer and other agents as the starting point. Then it will adopt a continuous process of organisation, rather than a hierarchical model set in stone.

The main factor is operating culture. Firstly we must give up the belief in ultimate, correct or findable solutions to all problems. The most dangerous thing is a management that claims to have all the answers. Building and defending administrative silos is the safest way of failing in one's basic task.

Decision-making and implementation are ever more strongly interconnected. The way in which we act becomes a crucial strategic choice. A leader's duty is to generate psychological safety, trust, a clear, collectively internalised direction, and meaning and substance for the work done. They are involved in creating shared significance and leading the individual and collective performance of all those in the community. Leading learning and utilising collective knowledge are becoming essential aspects of leadership. Leaders who have sought their positions for the sake of power are probably in the wrong place. The leader's identity is increasingly that of a servant: their task is to provide metaphorical wind cover for professionals as they carry out changes.

Changes cannot be achieved by telling someone else they have to change. This can only happen via intuitive perception and intrinsic motivation. Few people want to be changed by others, but many want to be involved in bringing about change. Experimentation, giving space, encouraging change processes from the bottom up, and setting an example with one's own actions create a basis for sparking the flame of internal incentives for change. Instead of a strong leader, we should aim for strong *leadership*, which is spread broadly across the workplace.

In a networked and systemic operating environment, leadership is spread even wider than that. It does not spring from fulfilling the leader's wishes, but from building the network's shared trust. The various armoire-pushers must be brought together to determine firstly what problem they are out to solve. After that, they must try to reach a shared understanding – through dialogue, listening, discussion and learning. Identifying and reinforcing a collectively agreed mission is essential in leading a network. Those with leadership positions must not have their own hidden interests at play, because that ruins trust.

In relation to the ten illusions, I wrote about the nature of wicked problems. Those unsolvable tangles containing mutually conflicting paradoxes are characteristic of networks and defy our natural yearning for control and solutions. Wicked problems cannot be solved with mind control techniques. We must surrender. Only giving up the idea of reaching a single, permanent solution can open doors for us to move forward. Therefore, leaders must be able to rely on the trust that has been built to get each agent to give up some of their own interests for the common good.

The skills needed by leaders are close to pedagogical in their approach, and the leader's identity is close to that of a teacher. The teacher's identity involves sharing all they know for the benefit of students. Traditionally, the leader's identity has often involved keeping their valuable knowledge to themselves, because knowledge is power and sharing it would reduce its value for the leader, thereby weakening their chances of rising through the hierarchy. This no longer works. Because there are no off-the-shelf solutions to certain problems, leaders must be able to engender a spirit of trust and collective development, within which agents can safely share their expertise for the sake of finding the optimal, unique solutions.

Just like a teacher creates a safe learning environment, a leader should create a safe environment and process for finding solutions. Learning and finding solutions are actually one and the same in a complex environment. Work and learning intermingle. Collective learning, development and culture can break down the cult of the heroic leader and the silo mentality in work organisations.

Leadership always takes place in a specific context and time, and that requires the capacity to discern what kind of leadership is needed just then and there. Shifting to empowering teams and leading functional ability, culture and people requires an in-depth redefinition of the leader's role. If you don't know where to start, you can always turn to your team and ask: "How can I help?"

Learning does not spring from having an experience, but from reflecting on the experience. Research has shown that someone who has done the same job for decades is not automatically better at it than one who started a couple of months ago. Turning a learned skill into routine is often wise in terms of personal resource use. Once we have learned to drive at driving school, we do not consciously improve our skills at it: we turn driving into a routine, so that we can think about other things while doing it. In creating routines, we can save the resources that are required by reflection and conscious learning, but, as a consequence, we may remain at the same level for years on end.

The change in identity or operating culture that takes place through learning is impossible without a change in perspective, a transformation. We cannot know in advance what we will achieve and, conversely, relinquish when we do that. It is not about absorbing information, but about renewal. That means unlearning some things, leaving previous learnings behind. Psychological and physical changes happen hand in hand. The shift in our perspectives takes place when certain synapses quieten down and others strengthen.

Identifying and rescaling best practices are common methods of action for communities and societies. Many things can be replicated and scaled, but the results that a social group obtains through learning are seldom such things. They are processes in which the participants have generated something unique through their interaction. Simply transferring the outcomes to a group whose members have not undergone the same learning process is not viable. They will not have committed to or internalised the solutions as part of their identity or shared culture. They will lack the learning achieved through reflection. A functioning learning process may be copied for wide use, but its outcomes cannot.

Conscious commitment is needed for development. An open mind, flexibility of thinking and action, and viewing feedback as a positive opportunity for development are keys to successful reflection. As Carl Jung said, "Until you make the unconscious conscious, it will direct your life and you will call it fate." Learning and bringing about change requires time and space for reflecting on what has been done and observed. It demands that the individual and/or group consciously pause to review what has happened.

This phase is often forgotten in our busy lives – we rush on to new challenges before learning from the past ones. We fail to learn, even when the learning materials are within reach.

Learning is slow. Educating a community is slow. In our black-and-white time we tend to rate slow things as bad and fast things as good. Even sleep, which is so important in terms of internalising learning, has become an obstacle for our greed. Anyone who has built sandcastles knows that it is faster to demolish than to build.

The Nobel Prize Winner Daniel Kahneman (2017) writes about two types of thinking, fast and slow. Fast thinking is an energy-efficient, intuitive way of reacting to things based on gut feeling. Slow thinking is an energy-consuming way of consciously working towards an outcome. Fast thinking from the gut often wins out. Shirking from people who are different is a manifestation of fast thinking, whereas understanding that diverse people are equal demonstrates slow thinking. Professor Jaana Hallamaa (2019) has written about the combat between *fast evil* and *slow good*: "Hate speech in the media, like any destructive action at its most typical, is a fast evil. […] Some of the virtues of the slow good are patience and persistence."

Our basic values of truthfulness, integrity, democracy, equality and freedom of expression are challenged in our time. They are values that demanded centuries – and innumerable human lives – to take root. Defenders of these values often succumb to being ashamed of slowness; these days, however, slowness is a quality of the brave, of those who are not afraid to tenaciously go against the grain, to dive into the uncertain waters of trial and error, to live under pressure from conflicting ambitions, to walk on the edge to discover new things, and who value trust, togetherness, presence and growth.

We must consciously make time and space for reflection. It should be turned into a ritual that is always within reach for our minds. It requires practice, because otherwise we fill all the empty space needed for reflection by staring at our smartphones. Throughout history, people have known how to create moments of reflection. These included the prayers and retreats into introspection and deliberation involved in religious practice. Similarly, feasts and parties can be seen as pauses in the annual cycle to celebrate the passing of time, stages in human life, rites of passage or special achievements. People get together to remember what has passed and, by thus sharing it, internalise it into the identity and story of individuals and the community.

Many organisations' review and self-evaluation practices serve the same purpose. They are an essential aspect of operational development. For evaluations to support learning and growth, they require psychological safety and commitment to good intentions from all those involved. If the starting point for evaluation is a power struggle, it does not work as a reflection tool: it will only serve for apportioning blame and seeking reasons for shifting power from one place to another. This is a problem of many public and political reviews. When things become personalised, the evaluation process turns into a power struggle, coloured by fear and hatred. Naturally, the actions of persons in the public domain should be publicly evaluated, but in today's culture of dialogue it tends to happen through black-and-white branding, praising heroes and lynching traitors.

Criticism is the most valuable thing we can give each other, when we do it with good intentions and empathy. This kind of criticism is becoming extinct, as it is being reduced into a caricature of itself, a tool for wounding and discouragement. The aggravating culture of the media, including social media, weakens the space and flexibility available for reflection and learning. Similarly, it reduces individuals' cognitive flexibility, because mutual accusations cause fear, mind-freezing and trauma. The fact that more and more local elected officials and members of parliament are quitting because they are worn down by today's style of dialogue is very worrying. What kinds of personalities will then seek out positions of trust? If lawmakers and citizens experience dialogue as a threat, these negative feelings will make us tend towards a more rigid society with tighter restrictions. We will have less tolerance for each other and will limit individual and group freedoms through legislation or social norms. The losers will be trust and creativity.

Taking a moment of reflection means adopting an external observer's perspective on one's experiences, and we need practices and forums that facilitate reflection. Reflection is like weightlifting for our learning muscles. At the same time it strengthens our resilience as individuals and communities. For individuals, it is about creating useful routines and rituals that reinforce becoming what we want to become and living how we want to live. It equips us for coping better next time, overcoming traumatic events and integrating them into our life stories.

Similarly, communities and societies must create forums and structures where psychological safety and goodwill are guaranteed and where experiences can be shared and conclusions drawn together, the aim being to improve how the community or society works in the future.

Learning as Universal Imperative

FROM OUR very first breath as humans – and even before that – we are beings that continually search for clues in our surroundings and adapt our behaviour accordingly. We learn all the time. The challenges we now face require an increasingly conscious attitude of learning. When the proportion of new things in our surroundings increases, we must also reinforce our ability to process and utilise them. This accentuates our skills in continuous, lifelong learning in diverse environments. A prosperous lifestyle is one in which we consciously learn from life along the way.

It takes a long time for a child to develop through adolescence into adulthood. We humans are complicated psychophysical beings, who take our time to mature into independent grown-ups. We are, above all, sociable beings. Our development of identity through social interaction is a slow process with many stages, and each of them intrinsically comprises humanity at its deepest – not just the expectation of something greater or more real. We all have certain sensitive periods of learning, moulded by evolution.

I took part in drawing up the World Bank's World Development Report for 2018, as a member of an advisory panel chaired by the UK's former Prime Minister, Gordon Brown. For the first time in the organisation's history, the report referred to education, and its analysis included both good and bad news. The good news was related to great progress in getting children into school. The bad news could be summarised as that being at school is not the same as learning. A large number of students – a majority in some countries – had not learnt even the basics of reading, writing and mathematics after five years in school. From a schooling crisis, we had moved on to a learning crisis. Learning poses a much greater challenge than that of simple physical presence at school.

One significant reason for children not learning at school is that they often lack skills in learning. They may suffer from problems with their basic needs in nutrition and care. The brain's adaptability develops through a suitable combination of nourishment and learning. Basic skills and preconditions for learning are built – or left unbuilt – in the early years. After that, education systems tend to reinforce the starting situation: those who are well prepared for learning receive support for getting further, whereas those with poorer skills get left behind unsupported, and will eventually drop out of the system.

Equal learning skills and education are the best methods for solving our global challenges. The optimal way of eliminating poverty, building the structures that guarantee basic security for citizens, and developing a sustainable and profitable economic structure is raising the whole population's education level. Finland is a good example of that. It has taken us (like many other countries) decades to achieve, but the outcomes are sustainable welfare and the ability to respond to national challenges. Education increases the resilience of individuals, local communities and national economies to cope with threats and difficulties. Equal educational opportunities enhance a society's cohesion and commitment to the common good.

We must find a way to guarantee all the children of the world the opportunity to receive basic skills in learning through early childhood education. It is about starting off on the learning journey – the stage at which it is still possible to give children equal opportunities for reaching their potential.

We waste a huge amount of unique people's competence with today's operating models. The developing countries' chances of seeing a better future are weakened by their educated population slipping away to the developed world. At the same time, those with the least education are displaced by war, famine and impossible living conditions due to climate change.

Learning as a lifestyle starts in early childhood, with the acquisition of skills in learning to learn. It grows out of being curious about stimuli and of an attitude of seeing new situations, emerging challenges and feedback as opportunities for progress and development. It is reinforced by conditions that push us towards conscious self-knowledge and self-improvement, and towards doing our best for the community. Every citizen of the world must be given opportunities for making learning into a lifestyle.

[This idea has been further developed since the Finnish edition and is examined in more detail in the Epilogue.]

Learning as Global Ethic

GUSTAVE SPETH, former Administrator of the United Nations Development Programme, once said that he used to think the top environmental problems were biodiversity loss, ecosystem collapse and climate change: "I thought that with 30 years of good science we could address those problems. But I was wrong. The top environmental problems are selfishness, greed and apathy… and to deal with those we need a spiritual and cultural transformation." Speth, an esteemed researcher in his own right, admits that this is something we don't know how to achieve.

In other words, we are discovering that solutions cannot be found where we once thought. We stand before a radical change related to redefining humanity, to societal resilience and to global survival. This process is likely to take decades. Our old, previously functional approaches and behaviours are no longer applicable, and we are starting to become painfully aware of that. We have not yet developed new approaches and mindsets. We cannot yet verbalise and instrumentalise what we are trying to understand.

Humanity faces a monumental learning challenge to secure our survival. We should inspire in each other and in coming generations the capacity to redefine humanity and to learn to act in an ethically sustainable manner in a complex, mutually dependent global reality.

We have evolved the power to destroy our living conditions and the survival of our species. That power also demands the wisdom not to use it. Our deep-set internal beliefs must be better synchronised with the challenges and limitations posed by our external reality. That will mean redefining "quality of life", "progress" and "growth".

Our objective must be the comprehensive well-being of humanity; prosperity as part of a prospering nature and culture. We must learn to live safely in uncertainty. Our biological and cultural development should progress fruitfully through interaction. We must shed civilisation's self-destructive tendencies, and recognise human strengths and weaknesses as parts of higher individual and collective self-knowledge.

The deep learning journey we face is global in nature because our major challenges are global. Tiny local changes can have huge ripple effects in terms of renewal, but the motivation for change must spring from understanding our planetary boundaries. This should also be the lowest common denominator for collective, global ethics.

The premises of the Universal Declaration of Human Rights still apply. We now also have Sustainable Development Goals that, based on the best available information, provide us with a direction and the actions through which we can safeguard the survival of our species and the prosperity of individuals and the planet. The question is how to build global ethics that will make us, the representatives of our species, identify with and act in accordance with the interests of global citizenship. Humans have always had and will continue to have many identities, but a 'global' identity must assert itself as one of them. It must be one that strengthens communities, defuses conflicts and permits as much diversity as possible.

How can a global identity be asserted, then? The steps taken thus far — providing information on the challenges to come, scaring people with threatening outcomes, publishing scientific data and making calls for action — have not had the desired effects. They have not always reached people's deeply held beliefs, even though awareness has increased. A learning cycle that would become internalised as action and a part of individuals' identities has not been triggered.

Could the solution be found in the idea of the Japanese garden? Imagine the whole world, and shrink it into a small space — a box on the windowsill, for example. Global ethical problems can similarly be shrunk down to the local level, reinforcing the actions of local groups that are already committed to the idea of the common good and to solving global issues. Downscaling global problems is as possible as upscaling local ethical models. Then we would seek solutions through emerging learning techniques. Learning and the reflection it entails provide opportunities for us to develop identity and assume responsibility for larger entities. This prepares us for systemic change from the very start.

Earlier, I suggested providing universal early childhood education as a way of demonstrating global accountability. We need credible global structures and actions that foster identification with global citizenship. We need deeds and symbols that create emotional connections between all the diverse agents who are already doing laudable things, creating new ways of thinking and coming up with innovations for a better and more sustainable world. A global team does not compete with anyone. Global ethics intrinsically involves the idea of the infinite game.

Global issues and the internal coherence challenges that are faced by individuals are not far apart; they are aspects of the same whole. Political systems examine the world's problems as external questions to which they seek external solutions. The links between the external and our internal growth are seldom discussed.

Sustainable development goals are individuals' internal growth challenges. The goals cannot be reached without shifting our worldviews and mindsets to a new level. Identifying and declaring this link would be radical in the original sense of the word – a return to roots – and would entail the creation of a new paradigm. It could have a healing effect on the cultures of action and dialogue of politics, as well as on its rules.

[We are now, at the time of publication of this updated translation, seeing this emerge in the burgeoning movement around the Inner Development Goals initiative.]

The agents of the civic society play a crucial role, not only in controlling the exercise of power by governments but also in generating global solutions and identity. There seems to be an unfortunate number of people who are ready to give up on the ideal of open society and live under the thumb of authoritarian power. Being woven into the cloth of our everyday lives, the benefits of an open society go unnoticed. Our rights and our freedom as individuals and communities to grow into our potential and seize the new opportunities brought by life can only be fulfilled in the reality of an open society.

We must execute a complete shift from an industrial growth society to a life-sustaining society. We stand before an era of transformation. It is not about doing things differently, but about having a whole different basis for what we do. That basis is not aiming for financial profit or winning the competitiveness race against other countries – or even stretching economic globalisation into the most optimal position by extending its value chains. The basis must be reinforcing natural assets and biodiversity, thereby diversifying risks and boosting the resilience of individuals, societies and the planet as a whole.

Learning as a Journey into Ourselves

"BEHAVE YOURSELF!" is something I was often told as a child. It meant be good, don't fool around, act like a person is supposed to act. In that environment, "behaving" didn't require explanation: there was a shared understanding of what comprised proper behaviour.

The external world has changed enormously in my lifetime. Inventions and technology have made life much easier since my childhood days of baling hay or trudging to an outhouse through knee-deep snow. Back then, the cutting edge of knowledge was represented by door-to-door encyclopaedia sellers. Through technology, we have been able to push this edge further out, and not only in terms of knowledge; new tools also afford us a greater reach physically and culturally.

We develop technology when we feel, as humans, that our reach is insufficient. We created the spade and the excavator as extensions of our hands; binoculars and telescopes allow our eyes to see further; while bicycles, cars and planes transport us beyond our own range. Technology makes up for what we see as our limitations and deficiencies. Artificial intelligence replaces humans' finite ability to process large quantities of information and to identify probabilities and patterns in data in order to draw conclusions.

Using technology is a social process. Innovation does not happen until our ways of working and everyday living change, turning new technology into a significant part of life. This is why the future is not primarily a technological or scientific development challenge; it is a challenge to humanity, democracy and fellowship.

If we believe that people must adapt to a future laid down for them by someone else, we will fail. That is not the way. A part of humanity's growing mental health struggles has emerged as a healthy reaction to developments that we consider to be wrong and that we have not been involved in causing. Genuine involvement could be a more effective cure for this than antidepressants.

Technology cannot, therefore, solve everything. Reaching further morally, mentally and spiritually comes down to ourselves. This is why investments into understanding humanity and supporting human growth are needed as much as those into technology. We need innovation for our human interactions. We are capable of creating tools for developing the mind, understanding reality and achieving shared goals; refining structures, roles and professions comes naturally to human culture. Why shouldn't we use this natural propensity for bringing people together, for building bridges that can help solve our global problems?

Throughout history, narratives have steered people's actions and lives. Our nature as social creatures is passed down the generations through stories, and stories help us disseminate and learn culture. They are built upon a piece of information or an emotion that is meaningful for us and packaged into an easily transmittable form.

Stories are like a sandwich of the human mind: all the essential ingredients are brought together into a compact, sturdy and easily portable format. The core content of stories does not need to be taught separately because it is contained within the narrative. A good story is stirring, and we know its core to be true even if we are unaware of it. Narratives move us, and therein lies their power and their peril: they can be used for good and evil alike.

Narratives help us to step beyond ourselves and to connect with the collective. They encompass an understanding of the essence of reality, a journey towards a desired outcome, and links to the listener's own life. Today's narratives have started to incorporate the idea of an apocalypse or endgame. We need a new kind of narrative that serves what we experience as meaningful and motivates us to make it manifest in real life. We need a narrative of humanity, of flourishing nature and an unending game, a narrative that brings us together on a global scale.

We live in meaningful times. The living environment we have created and the problematic chains of events this has led to demand transformation from us. Renewal implies the systematic and systemic utilisation of our human strengths.

Some of the individual risks I described at the beginning of this book may well be solved through investments into technology and use of market mechanisms. However, in order to prevent the dangerous cocktail brewed by these individual crises igniting each other, those means are insufficient.

Transformation requires the ability to integrate all the specialisation and deep learning that we have managed to accumulate, on a more complex new level. This applies to human awareness, as a web of our senses, corporality, thoughts, emotions, memories and minds. It applies to understanding mental development as an aspect of human relations, as the interconnectedness of our close circles, our communities and societies, with and for humanity and the more-than-human world.

On a cultural level, it applies to reinforcing the shared language and the human interaction already present in academia, the arts, religions, beliefs and old and new narratives. We must not throw away what we have achieved through partitioning and sharing of tasks, and we need not relinquish the strengths and diversity of perspectives provided by specialisation. Instead, these strengths and perspectives must be brought together to achieve more comprehensive and better understanding and communal wisdom.

Many basic elements work in similar ways at the individual, community, societal and global levels. Personal self-reflection, communal dialogue, social renewal through portfolio thinking, planetary systems theory and global ethics are all based on contextualisation, adaptation and learning. The various levels support each other and are interdependent.

A mind with a diversity of connections is flexible and can function in various situations and challenges. A community with diverse connections is adaptive, capable of recovering from crises and surviving through change. A society with diverse connections is open and functional and will not descend into chaos or regress to a black-and-white worldview when encountering a crisis. A global community that strives to reinforce the prerequisites for life and to look after biodiversity will have less concentrated risks and an improved ability to recover in the face of unexpected disasters.

"It was John Dewey's belief that new things could only be born out of people coming up against the unknown and processing it collectively."

Ordinary citizens must be brought into partnerships between the public, private and academic spheres. A pioneering position cannot be achieved by suppressing critics, but by taking into account the threats of which they warn when developing innovations. Empathy is what links narratives of fear and success. It is already happening: new models of communal decision-making, influencing, mediation, participation and dialogue are springing up like mushrooms after rain. And like mushrooms on the forest floor, they can be hard to spot from afar but abundant once you know what to look for. Communal wisdom is found in small, practical solutions, but unlike hate speech and conflict, they seldom reach the spotlight in public discourse.

It was John Dewey's belief that new things could only be born out of people coming up against the unknown and processing it collectively. In the future, many things will be unknown to us all, so the only alternative is to handle them together. We need tools and understanding related to how to be human together. How can we live in a way that achieves good things not just for ourselves but also for others? How can we make satisfactory choices in life that are also sustainable from the perspectives of other people, future generations and the environment? How can the tensions sparked by people's different points of view be defused and turned into a resource? How do we achieve consensus on what facts to use as a basis for decision-making? How can we reconcile sets of values that are fuelled by opposing each other? How can we grow together in harmony?

These are difficult questions. An even more difficult question is one that we face here and now: the challenge of our time. What would the eight billion people on Earth do if they had to ensure the continuation of life and opportunities for prosperity for many generations into the future? If we immersed ourselves into these questions from an ethically sustainable perspective, with good intentions and with the same scale of investment that we have sunk into altering our surrounding world for the purpose of increasing our economic wealth, the world could become a better place for all of us, for the environment and for future generations.

It will demand time and energy, but less so than it would take to repair the damage caused by inaction. It will lead to failures, but we can make progress by learning from those.

We have been incredibly efficient in turning natural resources into economic ones. Now we must consider how to turn our economic resources back into natural ones. We have to grow out of our "Mother Earth" ideology – the idea that we are children who must exploit their mother's resources as best they can to prosper. Growing up means shifting to a more balanced relationship: one of maturing together, where giving and receiving are reciprocal and facilitate evolutionary becoming instead of simply existing.

We must prove that we are not a dumb parasite which, by killing its host, simultaneously destroys its own living conditions. It is up to us to demonstrate that we can live symbiotically in the ecosystem that we have chosen and adapted into our own. It is possible for us to ensure that future generations can experience the wonder of life, make their own choices and live with human dignity.

Instead of using technologies to reinforce our weaknesses and deformities, we must apply them to eliminating these. How wealthy are we to have all the world's knowledge, all the pinnacles of human thought and wisdom – from ancient myths to the most recent insights, scientific findings and artistic creations – at our fingertips?! Our chances of generating well-being and prosperity, of reinforcing humans' spiritual growth and humanity's welfare in unprecedented ways, are better than ever.

We also have significant institutions and systems in place that can take care of implementation. Our financial, political, national and civic institutions and communities are highly capable of executing the desired changes, given the right circumstances and having made the correct choices.

We have all the prerequisites for learning to act in the moment, such that in the next moment there will be more alternatives to choose from. That is genuine sustainability: taking into account all the people in the world and all the unborn generations and their opportunities for thriving in life.

What can I do? Having agency is crucial. In our individual-centric world it fills us with angst to be personally expected to take large-scale, redeeming action. The pressure is too high and this manifests itself as anxiety, depression, denial or projection onto others. There is always someone else who should be in charge of achieving change. Those with access to the world's wealth: billionaires? They appear to have too much to lose personally, were they to effect change. Decision-makers who have more power than us? They, in turn, seem too caught up in the challenges of being re-elected to take unpopular action. So who will bring about change?

Our focus must shift from the individual to the communal. Individuals matter as part of a community; each of us has our purpose to fulfil. Fulfilling it to the best of our ability, with good intentions and striving for truthfulness is enough. We don't need individual superhero stories. Fulfilling our purpose is possible within the scope of our available resources, capacity and starting points. It is enough. What matters is to awaken to the need for change and to realise that there are better ways of being.

Finding a solution requires that we turn our gazes inward, onto our own selves, for therein lies the crux. In each of us. In the instances that we are able to engender, here and now, when we have the will to achieve it. One instant at a time: a brief one at first, then gradually longer ones. Instants of growth and learning, of human development. One good thing at a time; first a small one, then a bigger good thing.

Self-knowledge and finding harmony between the self and our surrounding reality demand honesty. We must live humanely, relying on the strengths that we possess: imagination, wonder, creativity, the ability to create significance, the capacity to achieve desired outcomes together. Utilising these strengths demands not only practice but also shared playfulness. The worst recourse is to resort to self-deception – to trick ourselves into believing that we don't know what we know, and that we can't do what we are capable of learning. We must face the challenges of our existence and transform ourselves into solutions. As the organizational leadership expert and MIT professor Otto Scharmer puts it, we must open our mind, heart and will to internal change, in interaction and in harmony with our surrounding reality. Then we will learn what is real. The story of creation continues.

This is a journey. Journeys take time. Contrary to the ideals of our prevailing culture, human spiritual growth is agonisingly slow, often painful and also exhausting. And yet it is both the correct and the imperative path for humans to take, as individuals and as a species. "Slow is smooth, smooth is fast," as the US Navy SEAL saying goes.

Internal spiritual growth cannot be rushed or forced. It does not happen according to the same logic we apply to making deductions or solving problems. It must take place viscerally and subconsciously. While growth may become noticeable at a specific moment in time, years of gestation may lie behind it.

When our minds are under strain, the wisest thing to do is to slow down and listen to ourselves, to perceive what is significant and what isn't; what is hurtful or joyful; what replenishes or drains our energy. When the intersections between external reality and inner mind become painful, the pain may be alleviated by touching things with our hands, finding connections with others, expressing things through our bodies or communing with nature.

What is essential in being human is to see oneself as part of a larger, wonderful whole, as a droplet in the temporal stream running from the past into the future, and in the continuously moulding and transfiguring substance of reality. It is marvellous to belong to the entity that has given birth to us and that will continue to live on after our passing.

That is the vision of humanity that I have upheld. I know it is flawed and incomplete; perhaps by the time this book is published I will have changed my views. That is part of the wonder of humanity: the ability to learn and strive to better understand things together. I strongly believe in a continuous cycle of learning, differentiation and integration. When we strive to be human together we gain new insight into ourselves and our surroundings, and the cycle of meaningful life is strengthened. We can continue our journey into the unknown with a more confident step.

hear my former politician self, asking whether an election can be won going down that route.

Slowness is a quality of the brave.

We are discovering that solutions cannot be found where we once thought.

The ability to combine the verbal and nonverbal, the exact and inexact, the measurable and immeasurable

Instead of a strong leader, we should aim for strong leadership, which is spread broadly across the workplace

This is a journey. Journeys take time.

Renewal always involves giving something up.

The Finnish expression for "who wears the trousers in the house" is "who decides where the cupboard stands".

We have been incredibly efficient in turning natural resources into economic ones. Now we must consider how to turn our economic resources back into natural ones.

Epilogue:

Global Challenges as Educational Challenges

FIVE YEARS after writing the first version of this book, and with wars around the world and the spectre of artificial general intelligence dominating our headlines, placing the blame on technology for our social and ecological ills is equivalent to blaming only the arms industry for the bombings of war. Although artificial intelligence and other technologies accelerate development, the most serious focus we should have right now is on the relationship between ourselves and our machines, and on what it means to be an ethical and empathic human in this era.

Under such conditions, the institutions created to bolster our humanity, defend our collective agreements and generate trust have been put on the defensive. The media has had to search for its identity after losing its gatekeeper role and reposition itself within the fierce competition of the attention economy. The universities have had to expend their energies fighting internal culture wars, boycotts and smearing, while science and expertise have been questioned, and defensiveness has taken priority over strengthening ongoing inquiry. Schools are struggling amid many accusing fingers in a situation where children and young people from increasingly polarised societies come to school in the morning with cell phones in their hands, and teachers have unwittingly become participants in a competition for attention. The loss of identity and legitimacy unites institutions historically in charge of helping us to make sense of our (mis)perceptions and build on our collective human learning potential to sense wiser pathways out of our current predicament.

Throughout history, the central question of what it means to be an ethical and empathic human has been understood well by different societies. There are concepts and terms around the world describing the human formation of becoming a good person others can trust, and who is capable of utilising the processes of knowledge acquisition, truth-finding and aesthetic perception, thus bringing the individual and the general into closer alignment. As a beloved child is called by many names, this phenomenon is called 'ubuntu' in parts of Africa, 'buen vivir' in parts of Latin America, 'bildung' in Europe, and 'sivistys' in Finland. Some of these terms have an archaic flavour, further proof of us almost forgetting something so essential about being human and a member of society.

So one of the key questions of our times is, what are the new institutional frameworks that will enable our collective remembering at this crucial historical moment? As the responses to recent COP gatherings and United Nations summits will attest, there is valid scepticism about whether the needed change will come from our current centralised institutional frameworks that emerged in the post-war period. As I mentioned in the introduction, the social technologies that we are now searching for need to be very different from the Bretton Woods agreements, and I am heartened to know of the many brilliant people all around the world working on this issue. Indy Johar from Dark Matter Labs sums up the design challenge well:

> *How do you build an organisation which is not organising for control but organising for learning and curiosity? ... Where the real work is to find out what the work is? How do you build an organisation which is able to operationalise into the*

unknown as opposed to operationalise and proceduralise the known? (Johar, 2024)

Thus, our global challenge is a learning challenge, which is also what I hope to have shown with this book. It is also the context in which educators, education providers, administrators and policy-makers have to lead the way – after all, learning is (or, at least, should be) our core business. In the face of great and growing complexity and uncertainty, we are asked to unpack the deep basic questions of what the purpose of education is, what are its final aims, and what is relevant to be learned in our times? Theoretical, evidence-based reflections are necessary, but not enough. Solutions need to be understandable and actionable, not only in top ranked schools, but in every school and educational context.

Artificial intelligence and other technologies also magnify the pressures of change that schools and education systems are experiencing. Existing curricula have a bias towards propositional, scientific knowing, which is the area where AI has the greatest potential to outperform us. The discussion around "21st century skills" has already lasted 30 years, and still we are struggling to take the first steps towards embedding those skills in everyday teaching and learning practices and in pedagogical solutions in classrooms. It is becoming painfully evident that the term "21st century skills" will refer to the fact that it will take a century to integrate these skills systematically and coherently.

As a species, we are uniquely positioned with an incredible collective ability to learn and adapt, and we need institutions that enable, value and direct this capacity to spark changes in the ways we look at the world, treat each other and treat nature (Mulgan, 2012).

Our new institutions need to embrace complexity. In a complex world, our responses must be embedded in an understanding of complexity.

This is not something that should be feared. My experience is that we humans intuitively understand the complex nature of life. It is our propensity to overcomplicate – separating, specialising, categorising, reducing, decontextualising – that makes things difficult to understand.

Our new institutions need to be intergenerational and co-created. Young people understand the dynamic and interconnected nature of the world. They are also eager and passionate to co-create and find solutions together. They have the energy, but not the experience, and that is what us older generations can offer them. We have to create a new version of intergenerational transfer, which is perhaps more about dialogue and collective sense-making than "transfer". Transfer is only a small part of that interaction needed between different generations. Just having had the gift of my first grandchild being born, the idea of intergenerational learning is very dear to me. This is about dialogue, in the sense of listening, living together, learning from one another without pushing KPIs or other metrics; coming together, connecting, living and sensing life as it flows.

Our new institutions need to be planetary in responsibility and local in responsiveness. In the section on Learning as Universal Imperative, I suggested a practical policy direction that would invite our global ability to respond – our responsibility. As many have suggested (Rifkin, 2009; Lovelock & Appleyard, 2019; Hagens, 2020), an increasing awareness of our intricate global interdependence calls us now to a species-level consciousness and ethic of care and reciprocity. This has been frequently recognised in historic 'universal' treaties and declarations, but they are too often detached aspirational statements of intent and empty promises. Like countries that are trialling direct investment schemes, like 'basic income' and climate adaptation funds, we need to start investing in real change, but on a planetary scale. It will not happen without decisive and tangible action. As we say in Finnish, it is time for the cat to stop circling the hot porridge!

As a magnificently diverse species, it is challenging to find a lot that we can *all* agree on. However, it is a near universal truth that we want our youngest humans – our precious daughters, sons, nieces, nephews, grandchildren – to have the best possible start in life. Investing in this foundation is a way to demonstrate and deepen our consciousness that everyone matters to everyone, that we are truly planetary. But in the true spirit of reciprocity, a planetary identity and ethic will only develop with proof that global structures make it worthwhile to try to influence and build a better world. We need to experience this reciprocity: because I, an equal global citizen, have received proper conditions and skills for learning from the global community, I am prepared to act in a way that increases the prosperity of all people and of humanity.

It is abundantly clear from the evidence that a person's first 1000 days on the planet are critical (UNICEF, 2023). A strong start is crucial for brain development and a robust foundation for "good health, nutrition, learning success, social-emotional development, and economic productivity throughout life." (UNESCO, 2024)

The responsibility for providing equal learning foundations cannot be placed on the shoulders of national governments alone. We need a strong global responsibility. That would simultaneously reinforce the achievement of some of the UN's other Sustainable Development Goals. It would place the responsibility for fulfilling those on the broader shoulders of more highly educated generations.

This would also be a way of transferring resources from developed to developing countries, thereby being comparable to development aid. It would build foundations for more extensive improvement of education system quality and equality in the developing world, as well as for lifelong learning. From the perspective of individual global citizens, i.e. children, it is not about receiving money but about respect for their human dignity.

I would like to propose the establishment of a "1000 days – Investing in Planetary Foundations" global fund to ensure that all c.650 million pre-primary school age children (Our World in Data, n.d.) around the world received their right "to inclusive quality care and pre-primary education, with special reference to the most disadvantaged children." (UNESCO, 2022)

This fund would provide early years support, universal in its reach, but locally responsive in its implementation, paid for by proportionate contributions from all nation states (based on the relative size of national economies) and venture capital from wealthy multinationals. In a similar way that industry is being called to "pay for nature" (Taylor, 2024), it should be beyond general taxation at the national level that responsibility is taken for investment in the future capabilities (and survival) of the human species – like stronger antibodies of the global Superorganism (Hagens, 2020).

I know at this point readers will be coming up with a whole bunch of reasons why this is unviable. I will leave room for your creativity by not listing them myself. Just remember that a lot of important things in the world were originally impossible.

The Covid pandemic proved that huge changes can be implemented when there is a will and an imperative to do so. We are starting to face another global imperative. Systemic change is necessary, and action is needed to reinforce our global citizenship. The weakening of world organisations must be turned around, and we would be wise to find global solutions in arenas beyond the economy and taxation. Every person's right to grow and reach their potential lies at the heart of global justice.

Our new institutions need to be relational, rather than transactional. We do our best to reach our aims as isolated individuals, and as a consequence we get a world nobody wants. We are blind to the sum of our individual actions. Take the example of personalised services. Everyone wants to have services and products tailored just for them. Customised mass production is now within our reach. But what will we lose in a world governed by the satisfaction of personalised needs? Our relationship with each other becomes transactional – a push in the already strengthened direction of individualism and selfishness. By bowing only to individual needs and desires, we neglect the well-being of the community. As long as we see the world as a place 'made for me', we are on a problematic path. While every personalised service or product might claim the noble intentions of more efficiently satisfying unmet needs, the sum total of billions of personalised services is a world that no-one wanted – an unhappy world of selfish, lonely, disconnected people. We should think twice about what we hope for.

Education needs to swim against this tide. That is the transformative power of education. I feel even more strongly today than when first writing the book in 2019 that now is the time to dare to think and act. Beneath the typical curriculum and assessment discussions, there are some radical – in the sense of Latin word *radix*, root – changes to be made. Our foundational ways of sensing the world need to be reconsidered. Otherwise, as a mountain stream always finds the same riverbed, our thinking follows the same route, which is causing all the problems we're experiencing.

How can we help the river find more sustainable routes to flow, and how can education contribute? I have used the ten illusions of the modern mind to shed light on the challenge ahead. When making sense of reality, to be able to fully engage and flourish in life, our main tools are concepts, words, language. They mould and steer our beliefs, values, aspirations and moral perceptions. To change course from the existential threats, we need to break the habitual patterns of thinking. Otherwise, how could we prepare young people to arrive at different answers? We don't have to create a new language to see the world differently, but we must utilise more diverse ways of expressing ourselves. There are plenty of examples in indigenous cultures and areas of art and faith that have found more sustainable ways of describing our relationship to nature, others and ourselves. The closer we are to the core of the ten illusions, the more we need to unlearn. We need to get rid of the perception that the language of the global north is the objective, realistic, neutral, true and right way of making sense of the world. Once we are capable of that, we are on the right side of history.

To assist in our global transitions, education systems should offer new ways of seeing, sensing and interpreting the world, to reconcile competing beliefs and values, to rebuild meaning in young people's minds and restore well-being. With constant change and unpredictability, the context in which we live is never stationary. The relative proportion of the predictable is decreasing as uncertainty increases. Our ability to experience our reality as it is, and to have an open mind to learn from it, becomes central. The inquiring mind makes us resilient and adaptive in the face of surprises. Learning starts when we dare to enter the unfamiliar territory and admit our ignorance.

Bibliography

Ackoff, Russell: *Russell Ackoff / Haynes Media Works*, 2010. Retrieved: https://www.youtube.com/watch?v=MzS5V5-0VsA. (7 November 2024)

Aittokoski, Heikki: *Onnellisten saari*. HS-kirjat, Helsinki, 2020.

Andersen, Lene Rachel and Tomas Björkman: *The Nordic Secret*. Fri Tanke, Stockholm, 2017.

Bar-On, Y. M., Phillips, R. Milo, R.: *The biomass distribution on Earth*. In Proc. Natl. Acad. Sci. U.S.A., 115 (25), 6506-6511, 2018.

Bateson, Nora: *Aphanipoiesis*. In Journal of the International Society for the Systems Sciences 1:1, 2021.

Baudrillard, Jean: *Simulacra and Simulation*. Semiotext(e), USA, 1983.

Brand, Stewart: *Whole Earth Catalog (WEC)*. Fall, 1968. Retrieved: https://monoskop.org/images/0/09/Brand_Stewart_Whole_Earth_Catalog_Fall_1968.pdf (7 November 2024)

Carse, James P.: *Finite and Infinite Games*. Free Press, New York, 2012 (1986).

Casino-García, A. M., García-Pérez, J., & Llinares-Insa, L. I.: *Subjective emotional well-being, emotional intelligence, and mood of gifted vs. unidentified students: A Relationship Model*. In International Journal of Environmental Research and Public Health, 16(18), 3266, 2019.

Clifford, Scott: *Individual Differences in Group Loyalty Predict Partisan Strength*. In Political Behavior, vol. 39: 3, 531–52, 2017.

Corballis, Michael C.: *The Evolution of Consciousness*. In P. D. Zelazo, M. Moscovitch & E. Thompson. [eds.] *The Cambridge Handbook of Consciousness*. Cambridge University Press, Cambridge, 2012.

Dasgupta Review: *The Economics of Biodiversity*. HM Treasury, London 2021.

Dehaene, Stanislas: *How We Learn: Why Brains Learn Better Than Any Machine... for Now*. Viking, USA 2020.

Dondi, M., Klier, J., Panier, F & Schubert, J.: *Defining the skills citizens will need in the future world of work*. McKinsey, New York, 2021.

Drummond, C. & Fischhoff, B.: *Individuals with greater science literacy and education have more polarized beliefs on controversial science topics*. In Proc. Natl. Acad. Sci. U.S.A. 114 (36) 9587-9592, 2017.

Dunbar, Kevin: *Problem Solving*. In W. Bechtel & G. Graham [eds.] A Companion to Cognitive Science. Wiley, New Jersey, 2017.

Edmondson, A. C. & Mogelof, J. P. *Explaining Psychological Safety in Innovation Teams: Organizational Culture, Team Dynamics, or Personality?*. In L. Thompson & H. Choi [eds.] Creativity and Innovation in Organizational Teams. Lawrence Erlbaum Associates, New Jersey & London, 2006.

Feldman Barrett, Lisa: *Seven and a Half Lessons About the Brain*. Picador, UK, 2020.

Frey, Carl Benedikt: *The Technology Trap: Capital, Labor, and Power in the Age of Automation*. Princeton University Press, Princeton, 2019.

Geertz, Clifford: *The Interpretation Of Cultures*. Basic Books, New York, 1977.

Hagens, Nate J.: *Economics for the Future – Beyond the Superorganism*. In Ecological Economics, Vol. 169, 2020.

Hallamaa, Jaana: *Hate Speech as a Form of Action*. In O. Vainio & P. Kärkkäinen [eds.]. Apprehending Love : Theological and Philosophical Inquiries. Luther Agricola Society, Helsinki, 2019.

Henrik von Wright, Georg: *Explanation and Understanding*. Cornell University Press, New York, 1971.

Henriksen, Dorte: *The rise in co-authorship in the social sciences (1980–2013)*. In Scientometrics 107, 455–476, 2016.

Immonen, Perttu: *Suomen rahvaan historia*. Atena, EU 2017.

Intergovernmental Panel on Climate Change (IPCC), *Special Report on Global Warming*. IPCC, Geneva, 2018.

Intergovernmental Science-Policy Platform on Biodiversity and Ecosystem Services (IPBES), *Global Assessment Report on Biodiversity and Ecosystem Services*. IPBES, Bonn, 2019.

Johar, Indy: *Boring Revolution with Indy Johar*. Curiosity That Matters - S01 / E04. 1 March 2024. Retrieved: https://app.springcast.fm/18593/ctm-4-boring-revolution-with-indy-johar (19 November 2024)

Kahneman, Daniel: *Ajattelu, nopeasti ja hitaasti*. [Finnish translation by Kimmo Pietiläinen of *Thinking, Fast and Slow*.] Terra Cognita, Helsinki 2017.

Kegan, Robert & Lisa Laskow Lahey: *Immunity to Change: How to Overcome It and Unlock the Potential in Yourself and Your Organisation*. Harvard Business Review Press, 2009.

Kegan, Robert: *In Over Our Heads: The Mental Demands of Modern Life*. Harvard University Press, 1995.

Keynes, John Maynard: *The General Theory of Employment, Interest and Money*. Palgrave Macmillan, London, 1936.

Kilpi, Esko: *Perspectives on New Work*. Sitra, Helsinki 2016.

Lovelock, James, and Bryan Appleyard: *Novacene: The Coming Age of Hyperintelligence*. Allen Lane, an imprint of Penguin Books, 2019.

McChrystal, Stanley, David Silverman, Tantum Collins & Chris Fussell: *Team of Teams: New Rules of Engagement for a Complex World*. Penguin Books Ltd, 2015.

McGilchrist, Iain: *The Master and His Emissary*. Yale University Press Publications, New Haven and London, 2019.

McKinsey: *Defining the Skills Citizens Will Need in the Future World of Work*. McKinsey & Company, 2021.

McNeill, J. R. & William H. McNeill: *Verkottunut ihmiskunta: yleiskatsaus maailmanhistoriaan.* [Finnish translation by Natasha Vilokkinen of *The Human Web: A Bird's-Eye View of World History*]. Vastapaino, Tampere 2005.

Mead, Margaret. *Culture and Commitment: A Study of the Generation Gap.* Doubleday, New York, 1970.

Mercier, Hugo & Dan Sperber: *The Enigma of Reason.* Harvard University Press, 2017.

Mulgan, Geoff: *Big Mind: How Collective Intelligence Can Change Our World.* Princeton University Press, 2017.

Mullainathan, Sendhil & Eldar Shafir: *Scarcity: Why Having Too Little Means So Much.* Henry Holt and Company, 2013.

Our World in Data: *Global child mortality.* n.d. Retrieved: https://ourworldindata.org/grapher/global-child-mortality-timeseries (7 November 2024)

Our World in Data: *Number of children under 5 years old.* n.d. Retrieved: https://ourworldindata.org/grapher/under-5-population (7 November 2024)

Packard, Norman H.: *Adaptation Toward the Edge of Chaos.* University of Illinois at Urbana-Champaign, Center for Complex Systems Research, 1988.

Popper, Karl. *Three Worlds – The Tanner Lecture on Human Values.* Talk delivered at The University of Michigan, 7 April 1978.

Plato: *Valtio.* [*The Republic*] Finnish translation by Marja Itkonen-Kaila. Otava, 1981.

Rifkin, Jeremy: *The Empathic Civilization: The Race to Global Consciousness in a World in Crisis.* J.P. Tarcher/Penguin, New York, 2009.

Rittel, Horst W.J. & Webber, Melvin M.: *Dilemmas in a General Theory of Planning.* Policy Sciences. 4 (2), 1973: pp155–169.

Rose, Todd: *The End of Average.* Harper Collins, New York City, 2016.

Salami, Minna: *Aistien viisaus.* Kustantamo S&S, Helsinki 2020.

Schmachtenberger, Daniel. *Development in Progress*. Consilience Project, 16 July, 2024. Retrieved: https://consilienceproject.org/development-in-progress/ (7 November 2024).

Snowden, David J. & Mary E. Boone: *A Leader's Framework for Decision Making*. Harvard Business Review 11, 2007.

Solan, Matthew: *The secret to happiness? Here's some advice from the longest-running study on happiness*. In Harvard Health Blog, October 5, 2017. Retrieved: https://www.health.harvard.edu/blog/the-secret-to-happiness-heres-some-advice-from-the-longest-running-study-on-happiness-2017100512543. (7 November 2024).

Tainter, Joseph: *The Collapse of Complex Societies*. Cambridge University Press, Cambridge, UK 1988.

Taleb, Nassim Nicholas: *Antihauras: Asioita, jotka hyötyvät epäjärjestyksestä*. [Finnish translation by Kimmo Pietiläinen of English original, *Antifragile: Things That Gain from Disorder*.] Terra Cognita, Helsinki 2013.

Taylor, Frederick Winslow: *The Principles of Scientific Management*. Harper & Brothers, New York, London, 1911.

Taylor, Luke: *'A big, big win': Plan to pay for wildlife conservation emerges at biodiversity summit*. In Nature, 04 November 2024. Retrieved: https://www.nature.com/articles/d41586-024-03609-6 (21 November 2024)

Tilastokeskus [Statistics Finland]: *Väestörakenne*, n.d. Retrieved: https://stat.fi/tilasto/vaerak (7 November 2024)

Tomasello, Michael: *Cultural Learning Redux*. In Child Development, Vol. 87: 3, 643–653, May/June 2016.

Turkki, Teppo: *Aasia haastaa valtio- ja demokratiakäsitystämme uudistumaan*. Sitra, Helmikuu 2015.

UNESCO: *Tashkent Declaration and Commitments to Action for Transforming Early Childhood Care and Education* (November 2022). Retrieved: https://unesdoc.unesco.org/ark:/48223/pf0000384045 (21 November 2024).

UNESCO: *Early childhood care and education* (17 September 2024). Retrieved: https://www.unesco.org/en/early-childhood-education/need-know?hub=70242 (21 November 2024).

UNICEF: *Early Childhood Development: UNICEF Vision for Every Child*. UNICEF, New York, 2023.

Vartiainen, Pirkko, Seija Ollila, Harri Raisio & Juha Lindell: *Johtajana kaaoksen reunalla. Kuinka selviytyä pirullisista onqelmista*. Gaudeamus, 2013.

Vervaeke, John: *Awakening from the Meaning Crisis – Intelligence, Rationality, and Wisdom* (Episode 42, November, 2019). Retrieved: https://www.meaningcrisis.co/ep-42-awakening-from-the-meaning-crisis-intelligence-rationality-and-wisdom/ (7 November 2024)

Vervaeke, John, Christopher Mastropietro & Filip Miscevic: *Zombies in Western Culture: A Twenty-First Century Crisis*. Open Book Publishers, 2017.

Virkkula, Simopekka: *Mikä nyt on vialla?* Helsingin Sanomat, 12 March 2021. Retrieved: https://www.hs.fi/paivanlehti/12032021/art-2000007851347.html (7 November 2024)

Zimmerman, Brenda, Curt Lindberg & Paul Plsek: *Edgeware: Insights from Complexity Science for Health Care Leaders*. VHA Inc., Irving, Texas 2008.